Through the Storm

The Mastel

Bloomington, IN   Milton Keynes, UK
authorHOUSE®

AuthorHouse™
1663 Liberty Drive, Suite 200
Bloomington, IN 47403
www.authorhouse.com
Phone: 1-800-839-8640

AuthorHouse™ *UK Ltd.*
500 Avebury Boulevard
Central Milton Keynes, MK9 2BE
www.authorhouse.co.uk
Phone: 08001974150

© 2007 The Mastel. All rights reserved.

No part of this book may be reproduced, stored in a retrieval system, or transmitted by any means without the written permission of the author.

First published by AuthorHouse 11/5/2007

ISBN: 978-1-4343-1214-3 (sc)

Printed in the United States of America
Bloomington, Indiana

This book is printed on acid-free paper.

Prelude:

Just a little prayer many of us lose confidence in prayer because we don't realize the answer:

1. We ask for strength and God sends us difficulties, which makes us strong.

2. We pray for wisdom and God sends us problems, the solution of which develops wisdom.

3. We plead for courage and God gives us dangers to overcome.

4. We ask for favors and God gives us opportunities

What are you doing with what God gave you?
(It's all about exercising your true mynd)

From Druce to you with love.

Chapter 1

Too Right to be Wrong
Will Death become me?
Death becomes You
Forgive a Fallen Angel..
Have Vision
Seasons, An unconditional True Love
When will you release me from pain?
Look both ways before you cross the street
My Eyez
Hurt Heart
Becoming Innocent
Unwanted
Broken Spirit
Destiny
Dear Black Man and Woman
Blessings
Spiritual
Stray Dog
We all revolve around the Sun/Son (Which iz God)
What If Today Was Your Last Day
Because of Mary
Dear Everybody/Leaving my Apartment
Realizing Death

Chapter 2

Me and My Black Suit
Judgment Day
What Is It Do You Really Want In Life?
Hatred
Can't Miss Every Bump in Tha Road
Lil Black Horner
When It's My Time…
My Sinz
The Little Lost Black Sheep
Reflections
Support for Married Folks
Support for Open Minded Mankind
Free
The Rare Jewel
One Try…
One Wife…
Lookin Through Shaded Windows
Never Saw it Comin
They Judge Me before They Know Me
As I look Into My Soul…
Don't Criticize Before You Open Your Eyes
Give God the Praise
Gratification with No gratitude
Have Hatred
He Died Tryin

Chapter 3

Love Love
Mistakes
Never Hard to Deal with God
Show Me Love
The Cancer Patient
The Special One
Through the Storm
I met Hatred Riding a Horse but Love picked me up in a Cadillac
Once Upon a Time…
Our Father (For kids & others)
Pains of Rain (School kids Prayers)
The Cause of my Effect part 1
Lyrical Insight (the 7th chamber)
Please Strengthen my Try
If You Rush Your Mynd…
Hatred Romantic #7
The Reason that I am
The Blanket of Love
Consideration 101
To My Own…
Blue Moon, Red Sky, Purple Sun/Son
How Could I forget about God?
I Broke My Own Heart

Chapter 4

Spiritual Felonies
Living and Dying @ The Same Time
The Faith and Confidence Killer
How Did I become Jesus?
Adversity
What!!!! are you lookin for
Why do Daddies Die?
Wait on God's will…
The Christian Relationship Story (example)
Search Your Soul…
The Pleasure in my Pain
Thank God for this Dream…(this is one of my visions)
Take Heed to God'z Advice…
It's Been a While…
Look Behind You 2 Find You
Building a House to tear it down
Y Iz Your Hat Red?
What Are You Doing with What God Gave You
Who will be the Hate-est
A Higher Love
Why
Thank God We made It…Part Two
Look What Your Hatred's doing…

Chapter 1...
Strength from within

Too Right To Be Wrong

Too right to be wrong, sounds like a title to an old seventies' song
But I already know most of you won't hear me until I'm dead and gone on
Too many people that I know and don't know have this problem of being headstrong
And when you tell them about themselves they swear up and down that they're right and you're wrong
Too selfish to respect positive expressions of another person's point of view
Is what I'm talking about this time applying or able to help any of you
I'm sorry I had to tell you this but stupidity has been going on a little bit too long
And I know with all the stuff I'm about to say to you, I'm too right to be wrong
You see we all tend to be too right to be wrong at some point in living a lifetime
But did you ever think after the fact that you were putting shade over an extremely potential shine
Something for your mind to chew on whatever ages you be and you just know that you are grown
Think!! To really listen to another person's feelings so you won't be too right to be wrong
Many of you still won't listen to me cause you're too right to be wrong right in this existence
I wonder why your thinking process won't speed up and re-think your first thoughts of a persistence of selfish ignorance
I gave you advice to help you with your problem so you could really see what was going on
But you told me "you don't tell me what to do, I'm too right to be wrong"
You didn't even wanna listen to the most advisory words from the bible
Instead you wanted to continue on you own righteousness within a selfish cycle
Some of my close people think that I'm too wrong to be considered to be right
I guess they're blinded with self and don't even have a sense of intellectual sight
When will you learn that your way is not always the way that things need to be worked
And that listening to a little good advice from other eyes of expressions can't and won't usually hurt
You see, you always will falter if you think that your vision is always the final decision
Especially if you lock yourself up in an all about you mental prison
Have an open mind it may help you in life to grow wiser and prosperously strong
Or is it you still can't hear me, closed mind, cause you're too right to be wrong

MASTEL JIKOLE
Copyright Mastel 2002

Too Right To Be Wrong (Summary)

Too right to be wrong
How long will this stuff go on
You run around with your self-made crown sitting on a self made thrown
It won't be long gotta tell you
Before your collapse of joy turns to failure
Won't learn tha lesson now ya full of depression from tha results that stupidity sells ya
When will you start to learn
Not listening good makes you burn
Too right to be wrong too weak to be strong and happiness you will never earn

MASTEL JIKOLE
Copyright Mastel 2002

Will Death Become Me?
PRELUDE TO DEATH BECOMES YOU

As I wake up some mornings, I smell a certain smell that's somewhat familiar in my air of breathing. It's the smell of death, because it seems like lately everybody that's family or poplar in society, is leaving. When am I to be next? I sit and wonder if I'm really going to wake up the next day or is this my last few seconds that I'm here existing. I think deeply about this I guess because a very popular star just recently died and right before she died that awful haunting smell of death was in the air persisting. It was the same smell that I smelt right before my Grandmother Mary was murdered in a home last July. And about 6 months before then, I had smelt it about a week before my uncle junior was about to die. Some people that kinda know me tell me that I'm crazy and that I have this crazy obsession with death or that I just need some serious counseling to look past my losses and pain. But I see it as just me expressing myself out of deep thoughts of life and death and how seeing life as death to come some day in the near future to me and then to you just the same. Its just reality and something that is meant for everyone not just me or all those that have already perished away. You were meant to leave when you were born, you were never meant to be here to stay. Its just that I choose to speak on it a little more than what others want to think about it because that smell becomes somewhat of a astronomical smell inside the conscience and sub-conscience confines of my mind. I have different visions of what the ending is like it is either going to be pleasant during sleep or if it's violent and unkind. Will it be gunshots or an accident of some sort that will take me away from my kids and loyal Dee lovers? Or will it be sleeping a good night's rest, soul not right with God, living ungodly like some of the long gone others. That kinda brings back to a question that was asked of me in prison of what are you doing with what God gave you? And what if today was your last day? Or last seconds living? Did you spend you last seconds getting high or drunk or having sex with an unmarried partner, basically did you die sinning? These things are on my mind because the first time I smelt death, I was high and drunk back in December nineteen ninety-four. And a real good close friend of mine was to die that night and he had been drunk about five or six hours before. It made me wonder if he had sobered up and did he kinda see his fate coming in a hurry when the car began it's twenty-two flips? Did he know about God and all the possibilities while he was taking his last alcoholic sips? Was he focused on living afterwards and did he kinda know that death was to become him then at his young age of twenty? What about his opportune time of living, did he think that time could never really be considered plenty?

Nevertheless my uncle had cancer and knew that his death was going to be one of those weeks or one of those days to take him from this earth. I seemed to be given a few examples that death becomes you eventually if you had experienced a mortal birth. There's no running away from it so try to prepare as best you can with God in mind and an afterlife of eternity. For it didn't take all these people that I've come in contact with that have gone on to know that some day soon death will become me.

Mastel Jikole

Death Becomes You

The captivation of life is so hard to contain
Many of us walk through life with a burdensome pain
Who is to blame for us not living long in this beautiful planet
Who is to blame if you are one of the ones that couldn't stand it
Death seems branded inside the mynd of me to you
And too much talking about just living would be a deadly untrue
Falsified existence is what we constantly see inside of this matrix
I mean life is real isn't it or it's suppose to be whatever you make it
I can't fake it I'm deranged probably because my mynd drifts on its own to see the future of nature
The ending of life was giving to all of us in the beginning by the creator
I know I talk about it a little bit too much for I guess what you call normal behavior
But I think why God does this in my sleep is because he had sent me a savior
A savior of all my sins and leader to a life of eternity
These are truly signs for me to straighten up because death becomes me

Death becomes you when you don't recognize the other side of life meaning you forget
That lives usually end with some type of abruptness without giving reality time to hit
See when you're dead then it's too late to take that move back or try that day again
Especially if you were living without God and you did die with a heart full of sin
Who do you think you will meet when your spirit and soul begin to slip away slowly from your body
Will God's band of angels meet you taking you to a paradise rejoicing a godly party
Will demons take your hand and pull you away like the images in the movie titled Ghost
Or do you even think of where your inner you goes when it forever leaves the human host
Do you think God will send Abraham, Isaac, or Jacob to say welcome to death let me direct you where you need to be
Or if you died violently will you still be in a bunch of pain and agony
Forever hurting because you were sinfully wrong when your passing snuck up on you and made death become so real and so true

Do you think I'm crazy now when I say that death, it becomes you
It becomes you in a sense because you begin to take on the very thoughts that's inside of my vivid descriptions
And I'm not the Godliest person in the world but sin is a sickness that needs a prescription
A prescription of life would be the ultimate answer opposing the ideal of becoming death
But if you leave without preparing your insides like you do your wills then your life becomes bad for your health
Mistreating yourself by abusing the life and body that God, to you, so generously gave
Shake you booty, drink, and smoke hard, screw everyone and become the devil's mental slave
You see all the things that are wrong to do that you like to do become an obstacle in your path
And you trip up over them every single time because you failed to sit down and do the math
The living here equation you + life =death −soul divided by spirit times everlasting vision squared
Are you visualizing with me now or not right now cause your thinking is alcoholically impaired
Or does false teachers or weed blind you or does your know-it-allness hold you back from a true understanding
Of that death makes it where you can't see the people you liked around you anymore but knowledge shows that some where in existence those people are still standing
Maybe not in a physical form but they do stand awaiting that great judgment day when Jesus is coming back to forever rule
Can you somewhat determine your destiny, will you be living where its hot or will you be living where its cool
One last pointer that I'm going to make before this short story poem ends and soonly becomes itself death
Is that black people need to stop fighting against each other trying to make it where its going to be nothing but a few black people left
And white people too need to stop hatred because when God made us he did make us different but we all came from the same ashes and dust
This is a message to, strictly for the wise, open you spiritual eyes and look with them because death becomes all of us

Mastel Jikole
Copyright Mastel 2002

Forgive A Fallen Angel And Hold My Hand (a thug's prayer)

Dear Lord, if I could only begin to say to you that I'm sorry, I believe things would be so much better
And I don't know if later on that I would be able enough to write you this type of letter
I've fallen, something that I know that you already have foreseen before me even telling you this
And it hurts so much because it seems that the evil that is in me still wants to exist
I remember when I was baptized into a family that was all about love and was connected through your son's blood
I also remember that seemingly that same day I was baptized into Satan's unblessed family of mudd
Not to put you two together because I do understand that you both are very opposite when it comes to being true and living
For every time I do wrong to Satan, he never says its okay and he is never forgiving
Instead it seems like he punishes me for wanting to follow you when I go astray from him
And the next time sin time rolls around seems like my shine becomes a little more dense and dim
He tries to drag me further under with all the lusts with no rewards and my soul for a ransom
He sends arrows to my weaknesses through Delilah to kill the soul of your new black Samson
Take my hair away from me to steal away all of my strength, my heart, my beauty, and my spirit
Lord I know I've been wrong recently and I pray to you hoping that you and the Father will hear it
My apologies for living the way that I've been carelessly caring on without my good spirit of God living
For I've forgotten that you told me that you would always be here with me and would always be forgiving
I wanted to be a warrior for you, a soldier for glory, a God loving king, but while I was running I slipped up and I fell…
Please forgive me oh Lord I pray to you because I have a little problem with too many wannabe-acting Jezebels

I am as sorry as Moses, David, Abraham, all of my previous ancestors, and all of your chosen leaders
Give me the strength to fight again like Samson so that I can make all the unbelievers become true believers
Believers of your existence and believers of your love, your wrath, and all of your heavenly kingdom's power
So that every man, woman, and children can maybe make it in without worrying, if in that final hour
This blessing that you gave me to write with a poetic sense of transcription I thank you for very deeply
Cause this is what sometimes kinda allows me to become tired, hesitant, and spiritually sleepy
Help me to fight this fight as you continue to spin my planetary axis from world to sun to my surrounding stars
And help me my God to be able to break away from all of these hellishly Satan filled presence of evil bars
Help me to not lie to your people but give them you, give them the truth with proof of me
Help heal me and my family's mind so that one-day we will be able to walk with you and the rest eternally
You already know that I'm a good soldier and that I want to do your will and obey your every living word
I just need a little help from you Father to fix and strengthen the wings of your fallen bird
So that I can fly again and soar strong in your guidance planting your seeds all over the different countries and land

Forgive me God your fallen angel and please…please I beg you to continue to guide me and hold my hand

Amen

Your son Druce.

Copyright Druce 2002

Have Vision

I'm in a position to give peoples thoughts some vision
Like a religion but they still won't listen to tha mission (have vision)
From a soul that needs cleansin outta tha cold bars of mental prison
Leave all the hatred thoughts alone and change your decision
How you livin thank God for givin you another chance for spinnin
Against other black men stop sinnin start defendin instead of offendin
With hate as the intention so you can arrive with me instead of not even makin it in honorable mentioned
What's your contention that has you so against God's humane invention that makes you think that your brother man not the other man needs some lynchin pay attention and don't mention how you're so lost in suspension Of where my mynd goes next which brain cell will I be pinchin or steadily pimpin as I'm inchin to let my soul rise pass tha disguise of fake guys who tell lies act like spies we all dies my soul cries to see peace finally come inside of my black eyes (have vision) to see love finally come inside of my white eyes (have vision) to see God finally come inside of my third eyes(have vision)

The Mastel

Copyright Mastel2002

Seasons,
An Unconditional True Love

Seasons are like reasons they change and they vary,
but unlike my love, there's no change that it carries
It's pure and it's total and the same without reason
but love of my kind won't change like a season
Sometimes you're baffled in a mysterious wonder
of why my love won't leave you like the season of summer
It comes and it goes unlike the love from my heart
for instance, in winter the cold will depart
A season it leaves you on a continual bases
but not my love it never goes different places
It's there for you always unlike the spring and the fall
because unlike seasons my love is there through all….Seasons!

BY DRUCE ROUZAN

When Will You Release Me from Pain?

I must be stupid or insane to even ask you this question
When will you forgive me of my sinz and stop all this testin
Because the struggles and hurt will always continue to strain
And force me to ask this question when will you release me from pain
Lord it hurts me to do all the things that you ask me to do
But I'm starting to know that the hurt that I feel is tha start of me being true
To findin my way to you and home with the livin lord and the Christ
And now I realize that these cold hearts just want to stab me with ice
The ice of Satan frozen in the hottest places of hell
I'm startin to feel you somewhat my Lord cause they keep driving the nails
In the wrist of my spirit and in the pits of my soulful feet
They hate me to be with you they hate that you make me complete
Lord I know that I stumble and forget that all of this is to train
So please pardon me when I ask you to release me from all this pain
Because you already told me that you will be with me until the ending of time
You said endure this struggle for a little while so that I can be yours with a shine
Sweet valentine for you only lord that's just me counting up your mercy
And I can't forget to thank you for forgivin the people that hate me and hurt me
I guess the phrase fits my purpose of no pain and no gain
Cause taking all of this world makes me want to forget it and go completely insane
Not even think about the times you brought me out of the valley of death
When everyone else was gone and it seemed like I was the only one left
Lord I guess to summarize this letter I've gotta thank you for this life, these lessons, all the glory when I felt so alone and disdain
Because you were there through all my misery of prisons to release me from these satanic flames
All the times that I loved people regardless if they didn't love me back
I appreciate that now dear lord cause not I see that you were there to take up their slack
So I say for the last time in this letter forgive me for all the times I've felt bitter and how my heart would at times complain
Cause you told me that not only now and not only then, but you would always release me from pain

Thank you, your little boy,

"Look Both Ways before You cross the Street"

Look both ways before you cross the street
You never know what you're goin to meet
You might meet yourself and oh what a treat
To find out that all of you ain't all that sweet
Why don't you even think before you speak
That's how you look before crossing the street
You're lookin at me and sayin why's he so incomplete
But look in your direction 1st before you cross my street
Because you also have wrongs that you didn't delete
BAAM!!! You got hit tryin to cross my street
You got hit by the lessons of sessions because you so wrongly seek
The faults of others tryin to make you strong and them weak
But make no mistake though cause GOD is real from bottom to peak
And while you're out there searchin, someone else is formin your defeat
Someone unknown to you now but whom has a unique physique elite
Someone who will show you about running so quickly out into other people's street
Into the street that's crooked by your vision thinkin we're suppose to dance to your beat
When will you stop to think that it's your fault to the people that you mistreat
You were the one that had the attitude thinkin that you were so right and complete
Now look at you, heart of concrete too cheap to meet defeat
Well this lesson is done for now and I hope I was able to teach
That in order to make peace, its inside you that you must 1st reach
I urge you everlastingly that these words that you do keep
And remember to look both ways before you cross the street

BY GOD AND D. ROUZAN

My Eyez

My eyes have seen love my eyes have seen hate
My eyes have been real my eyes have to create
My eyes have seen death and my eyes have seen birth
My eyes see tha sun my eyes see tha earth
My eyes see tha moon my eyes see tha starz
My eyes saw freedom, way beyond the bars
My eyes have seen violence my eyes have seen peace
My eyes saw incarceration until a tyme of release
My eyes have seen black my eyes have seen white
My eyes have seen darkness my eyes see tha light
My eyes have seen good my eyes have seen bad
My eyes have been happy my eyes have been sad
My eyes have seen race my eyes they see colors
My eyes see tha prejudice of white menz against tha brothers
My eyes have seen strength my eyes have seen pain
I've seen the strength of a wise man and the pain of tha slain
My eyes have seen joy my eyes have seen hurt
My eyes have seen relaxation my eyes have seen work
My eyes have seen plenty my eyes have seen great
My eyes have been hungry and have had to wait
My eyes have seen straight people my eyes have seen fakes
My eyes have seen brothers my eyes have seen snakes
My eyes have seen wrong, they tymes looked astray
They also have seen wisdom to choose a better way
My eyes have seen evil and have viewed with tha devil
My eyes have seen God, tha Bible, and thoughts made me another level
My eyes have seen struggle, shame, and Lord knows, hard tymes
My eyes have seen miracles that tha good God shines
My eyes have been high and ridiculously drunk
My eyes have been brave and sometimes even became a punk
Now to end tha story of my eyes through tyme came wise
These eyes had to learn about truth and these eyes already knows lies
They know a lot of things from crying tears to being filled with glee
They predict the sequel of slavery but they see through God that I am always free

My Eyes

Mastel Jikole

Hurt Heart (A Lesson in Apology)

There are some things in life we as humans sometimes forget and forsake
We cannot recognize sometimes that we are mankind and we always make mistakes
Mistakes of the like of the word HURT
Sometimes we do it to someone when not thinkin of what we blurt
We forget what we say to others without having any type of concern
But when others relate with us differently that's when you're suppose to learn
It's suppose to hit you and make you think....Finally, I understand why he's acting so differently
I've hurt him without even considering what ill-favored things that I have spoken
I've said some ugly things with no emotion to leave him probably heartbroken
What must I do to make things right between us ever again
Should I just say that I love you and forget all about his pain
Or should I do something nice to get his mynd off of that wrongness that I have done
Then will he forgive me and once again we'll be like one
Naw you're right, I can't do all that tryin and think that I have won back his favor
I can't give him weary attempts to want his forgiveness for my behavior
I must do what's right and fair and what seems to be so hard for me to be
I must talk to myself and break myself down to say the 2 God given words

I'M SORRY.
(A Lesson in Apology)
Mastel Jikole

Becoming Innocent

Eu·nuch (yˌ"n...k) *n.* **1.** A castrated man employed as a harem attendant or as a functionary in certain Asian courts. **2.** A man or boy whose testes are nonfunctioning or have been removed. -- **Eu"nuch·ism** *n.*

Matt 19:12
12 For there are some eunuchs, which were so born from their mother's womb: and there are some eunuchs, which were made eunuchs of men: and there be eunuchs, which have made themselves eunuchs for the kingdom of heaven's sake..
KJV

BECOMING INNOCENT SEEMS SO HARD AND SO FAR TO ACHIEVE
BUT THERE IS A WAY TO REACH IT THAT'S IF YOU ONLY BELIEVE
THAT THERE IS A GOD THAT WILL WALK WITH YOU WITH THRU THIS HUMANISTIC PAIN
YOU MAY THINK THAT YOU ARE LOSING SON BUT KEEP IN MYND IN THE END YOU WILL GAIN
THE UNDERSTANDING THAT THE DEVIL HAS BEEN AFTER YOU FOR SEVENTEEN YEARS OR MORE
AND HAS PUT IT IN YOUR MYND THAT YOU PHYSICALLY NEED TO SCORE
IT MAY EVEN BE SCIENTIFIC WITH YOUR BODILY HORMONES AND ALL
BUT LOOK AT THIS WAY YOUR STANDING FOR GOD SO HOW CAN YOU FALL
YOUR FATHER IS THERE SO GURD UP YOUR STRENGTH AND REMEMBER GOD
CAUSE THE EVIL THAT SURROUNDS YOU IS GOING TO TRY EXTREMELY HARD
ITS GOING TO MAKE YOU CRY AT TIMES AND YOU'RE GOING TO WISH THAT YOU NEVER TRIED TO TRAVEL THIS ROAD
BUT ITS BETTER FOR YOU, I PROMISE THAT, THIS BURDEN YOU UNLOAD

IF YOU NOTICED EVERY SINCE YOU WERE 12 THE BIGGEST PROBLEM THAT YOU HAD WAS THIS TYPE OF TEMPTATION IT ALWAYS STRAYED YOU AWAY FROM GOD THRU ANY AND EVERY SITUATION
<u>YOU</u> COULD NOT KEEP THIS UNDER BECAUSE IN YOUR WHOLE ACTUAL LIFE THIS HAS BEEN YOUR WEAKNESS TO SATAN
ALONG SIDE OF NOT BEING ABLE TO BE PATIENT AND HAVING SATAN'S WORKERS TRY INFULTRATING
BUT BELIEVE ME ITS GOING TO PAY OFF IN THE END OF TIME IF YOU GO ON AHEAD AND MAKE THIS DECISION
NO LONGER WILL YOU BE INCARSARATED IN PRISON BUT YOU WILL BE ABLE TO STRENGTHEN YOUR VISION
SO RE-READ THIS LETTER OVER AND OVER AND REMEMBER THAT IT'S HEAVEN SENT
CAUSE THIS ROAD IS HARD BUT YOU ARE TRYING TO BECOME INNOCENT

MASTEL JIKOLE

UnWanted

Through all that has transpired, I still want you. I just wonder, why are you treating me like a brand new bag of chips that you at one time considered your favorite? You couldn't resist my flavor. You needed to have me seemed like all the time and I just wanted to know why….why do you not want me any more? Is my flavor sour to you now, am I not fresh because you let me jus sit on your shelf untaken and not even give me a thought? Maybe you've chosen a new flavor and that new flavor has you so captivated that I'm really not even yours anymore, that I'm just a has been to you. Well whatever made you not want this rose that I gave you anymore, I apologize deeply that I wasn't able to be that initial flavor that you firstly tasted that you just had to have all the time. I apologize to you deeply for my flavor not being your liking any more. Nevertheless I tell you this…..that others will taste the flavor that you turn away and I will make myself available everyone.. it's okay because the very flavor that you once liked and turned away will exist without you, cause God is real. The taste that you had that you now do not want anymore will be tasted by and loved by others. They will want my flavor even more than you did when you wanted me firstly. They will also keep that yearn without forgetting about all of our first ness of everyday wanting. I just hope that it not too late for me to be able to change your heart. That it's not too late for you to taste my flavor again forever. My love will be forever yours as log as you <u>want it.</u> Please don't make me the unwanted, for I want you to want me. I want us to be together in heaven soon. If you choose other wise, I'll just have to accept it and go on, for I know that there will be mercy on the unwanted. As a matter of fact blessed is are the unwanted, for God wants all. Jesus!!!, THE UNWANTED.

By Mr. Rouzan

Broken Spirit

I can't believe it, a door once closed is now open
A spirit so happy is now broken
Broken from turmoil, confusion, and frustration
from all the painz of life and different situations
Mynd elevation still my surroundings they seem so gloomy
and for doubtful wordz that stab my heart gets so roomy
Then I say to myself "Man" these are part of the blessings
that you asked God for when you were in praying sessions
You said strengthen me Dear Father please make me strong
and he gave you plenty adversities to see if you could get a long
Struggle young man fight hard and keep on copin
and don't let the ruffness of Satan get your spirit broken
Never mynd what people say that may hurt you to your heart
The way they beat you the way they treat you, you won't get torn apart
Just believe in God, the truth, and the Savior
Cause you know he is your friend that will heal you from the cut of the razor
Eli, Eli, Lama Sabachthani
was the same thing Jesus said when they hurt him and he gave a cry
He said Father Father just as I do
whenever I am hurt and I feel so sad and blue
God!!! I mean Daddy please take this thorn out my side
just as you did for Paul when he was hurt and he cried
Please set me free from all this hurt and this pain
and let the sun shine to dry up all the rain
And Daddy said boy why don't you ever listen
What you suffer now iz what makes you a Christian
So go head on and suffer right now cause when it's over I'll give you a token
cause no matter what someone said, your spirit was never broken

Thank you God for showing me this.

Your son, Druce

Destiny

Destiny iz a atmosphere that iz alwayz reached through tyme
Tha destiny for criminals iz a jail whenever they do crime
Destiny for tha righteous iz known to be tha place heaven
You will receive that destiny once you've reached the number 7
Sometimes destiny is considered to be a perfect love connection
And sometimes stoopid destinies just create a sexual session
At tymes a never-ending romance seems to be my good destiny
Tha creation of life and love with a complete ecstasy
To be blunt with my knowledge as I cast you a spell
My destination at one tyme waz a inside a home cell, I mean a jail
Might as well cause I waz so destined to fail
But the God changed my mynd and made my strength to prevail
So now it iz known to me that destiny can be changed or rearranged
It can be planned if wise or condemned tremendously if stranged
Tha point of tha matter iz that a destiny can for a while be traveled
Your bed can be made of roses or your lifetime can be graveled
I choose tha soft road with truth and peace as tha recipe
Thank God for Jesus and Drece I finally found my destiny

Mastel Jikole

Dear Black Man and Woman,

I am very concern about you and your mental capabilities and how far you let them expand and to which direction of degree. Does your thought pattern excel. When will you wake up and realize that the whole existence of living is just that, living, and all of the misconceptions that you have of how the importance of so many irrelevant matters of black life cannot assist in giving a true life of living? No I'm not condemning my existence as a black man, no I would never do something like that, I just simply say that we intend to focus on things that are not too beneficial to our existence, things that can enhance or push us to do things that we deeply know are a negative traditions to our race. Instead we should do things to break the normal weeded up, drunken, and drugged up mynd of the weekend. Go ahead and ask yourself a dumb question, why. Why do you do the things that you know are very harmful to yourself? What benefit does getting high, drunk, or twisted bring to your soul, your inner spirit, your beauty? Are you imagining the goofy feeling of being lit or slizzard to be some great feeling? Or what about sex with someone that you don't anticipate on loving or seeing tomorrow with marriage plans? How deep is your mynd? How smart is your understanding? How dumb do you sound when you create the hallucination excuse to make yourself believe that you are justified by your sinful or immoral wants? Why is it so hard for you to swallow good advice when it is given to about your faults in life? Tell me, where's your life?

Mastel

Blessings

Tell me something new, why are you feelin all sad and blue?
Did God not give love to you or you just need something to do
I guess you're so bored and there's nothing else in your mynd
But ungrateful visions that make your blessings hard to find
You really don't need to find any blessings they're right in front of your eyes
But you gotta 1st humble yourself so that they can be recognized
Did you ever think how many suffer and don't even have a home
I guess you don't count your blessings enough until they are all gone
Sister girl let me tell you what thanks is all about
It's about thanking God for everything even if it's as sour as a kraut
Cause both good tymes and bad are very good to the soul
They allow you to go through life to learn the meaning of control
Sorry so short but I gotta close my poem and I hope that you've learned some type a lesson
The lesson of not thinking about complaining before you 1st count all your blessings

Count your blessings, please?

A poem by Maztel

Spiritual

When I was in jail all things came to pass
Realization that life never last
Here today said yeah gone tomorrow
Then comes the tears to seal all tha sorrow
Grief in the heart makes hurt so intense
Pain so fierce that I need love to rinse
Hurt so great only love can ease
To cure the painfulness of a sorrow disease
Of long lost friends families and all
Peace to L.G., Jr., and Mary we had us a ball
Smoking mad izm yeah I be in tha wrong
But that don't stop me from knowing God all along
One valuable lesson that I learned in jail
That life's too precious for us to play dare
Pass it on to the rest of these people in this God given nation
And to respect yourself as one of God's creations
Throughout all things that remain material
Focus totally on the stuff not physical
I thank God for tha life that I lead as a lyrical
Cause I'll be soon dead and gone and my mentals are spiritual

D. Rouzan
Copyright Mastel 2000

Stray Dog
Intro

Today someone that had a concern about her husband's sex life approached me. There was also a concern question of what the husband did in lue of the sexual intercourse that his wife deprived him of since whatever time of their decrease in sexual intercourse. The first thing that came to the person's mind was that the husband had to have been doing something to release himself sexually since they were not having intercourse on a regular basis. Now when talking about this subject, as well as other subjects relating to the poem to follow, a few conclusions can be made such as masturbation, adultery, visiting strip clubs, or viewing pornography. There are probably other conclusions that can be made but I just wanted to introduce a little bit of what inspired me to write this very controversial piece. There was also another person that had something that inspired this long awaited poem titled Stray Dog and that other person is who really inspired this piece but the most recent person made the poem definite. Welcome to the poem.

Stray Dog

Once upon a time there was a dog that was loved and accepted by its owner
The dog would run free around the town but was always a homer
The dog came home everyday because its master feed it and gave it love in every way
Not knowing that if you stop the feeding and loving that the dog would go astray
The dog kept coming home regularly like on time clock work
Then the owner start slacking and the dog felt neglected and hurt
So the dog stuck it out with the slacking waiting for dinner to always arrive
But when the owner got too busy to love, the dog still had to survive
So the natural instinct of dogs is to go find the necessities of living else where around
Even if it meant that the dog had to go all over town just to get down
There was always someone else willing to throw the dog something when those times were ill and hard
Others that probably wanted to become the dog's new owner and do the right job
The dog was in need just like the owner was for things in life
So the dog turned stray for necessities but not to be trife
Now tell me can you really blame the dog for going and becoming a stray
For the owner left it stranded, hungry, and in dire need everyday
The dog would come home faithfully if it knew that good love was coming its way
So tell me, why are you trying to make your dog go astray?

By D. Rouzan

Copyright Mastel 2002

We all revolve Around the Son/Sun (Which iz God)

Who would believe this that this brother his name iz Jesus
Would come to this planet to heal this world's diseases
To save exploding planets and all of the fallen stars
Put us back in the orbit to spin up on the axis bars
Revolve around each other like bullets inside a pistol
Until it's our time to be blasted ejected like a missile
Will I be next to pass on or is it the next bullet's turn
To be hit by the firing pin explode and be burned
Or be saved for later on talking eternal salvation
God and Godson forgive me for my sinful situations
And all of the battles that go on within my heart's mynd
And how the devil blinds and I become one of his deathly kind
Don't wanna miss the revolution as I evolve to become one
And acknowledge the living revolving around the sun/son
Forgive me dear God cause this life living is very hard
We all revolve around the Son/Sun which iz God

As my mynd travels it seems like its tyme for me to battle
Tha fakes and wannabes when they meet up with my shadow
Kill all tha hassle cause I got me dimensional flow
With multi-dimensional run like Jet Li when I go
From your dimension to mynd whatever type or kind
I tell the story like the sun/son see I try one shine
If I was the sun/son I guess I have to tell a lot of stories
On how using me as the source is something mandatory
For the eternal existence cipher traveling through tyme
No polish is needed cause my living thoughts are tha shine
I'm incredible cause as the sun/son I've seen me everything
I also seen the reign of life and death of kings and bling
I saw the real murders that was concealed from other's eyes
I saw the beginning of tyme I've been in tha blue skies
I've seen things from births to folks getting killed and robbed
Cats living hard do slob and keep losing their job, God
Help us to continue on cause there's no other way out
Let me understand your resolution before I revolve out

The Mastel
Copyright Mastel 2002

What if Today was my Last Day

What if today was my last day? How would you treat me
Would you treat me with love or would you treat me indecently
Hurt my feelings was that our very last thoughts of us
Was our last conversation a fight or a fuss did I cuss
Or did we share a special moment filled will laughter
Were we in tune spiritually eyes focused on the master
What comes after the final chapter I'm gone physically dead in the grave
Does tha pain that exist inside a you become or make you a slave
You rant and rave cause your heart is so regretful and guilty
Is it because of what we did last or do you really miss me
Love me now in God's day while the time still remains
Cause it might be your last day and you could go with a bunch of stains
Stains that could hurt for a lifetime after
Why won't you hear me before the last final chapter
Why won't you spend the last time remaining showing love to you, me, and all
I'd hate to see you take that long eternal fall
Let's end things with a strong beautiful God's prayer
Cause I most definitely want to see you up there
In the heavenly skies where there's no more tears, cries, and pain
Where there's no more struggle to exists and to survive with strain
The message is to treat me as if you were leaving without any sense of stay
In the manner you would want me to treat you if today was your last day

What if Today was your Last Day
(Adapted from the 3rd letter to Junior)
By D. Rouzan
The Mastel
Copyright Mastel 2002

Because Of Mary

As my mynd rages against the sea of understanding my heart is filled with joy
Because of my baby Mary little Brenda made a boy
Because of my Mary I write so destined to you
And I'm trying very hard not to let my writings be filled with rue
If you've read my work you already know what happened to my Mary
And you probably know how things in life can vary
They vary from love to knowledge to compassion to being loving and kind
Respecting and showing true love to others is the only way to have any type of peace of mynd
Because of my Mary my mynd has been prompt to give you people some of us
Something that can probably be used by you and yours to help you stop tha fuss
The fuss of problems that are always trying to pull you down and have probably you and your mynd so incarcerated
If you would look through our eyes then most of you problems could possibly be eliminated
Or do you like trouble, shame and a extremely miserable upside down world
Are you a stupid boy or are you a stupid girl
Your life was made simple but it was you who complicates it
That's why your heart cries all these tears and feels no love cause it's cold and naked
When will you take it the advice I give you about not complexing matters and making things on you worst
Or are you one of those stupid ones who wants to be spit on when they take you out the hurst
Then again are you a stupid one whose vision is taunted by any of these worldly illusions
If so then allow me some time for a mynd intrusion and revolution
You have too much pollution in your mental cup of tea
Too much confusion for your eyes to see
See bigger and better things that can allow you heaven and glory
So why do you think that complicating your life is so you and mandatory
Take away yourself from picking arguments over something that's so petty
If it's not about life or death then your mind really isn't ready
Ready to learn from the mistakes that you live tryin to fight and keep up mess
That's why you're miserable cause you keep bringing your own self stress
It's not me or anybody else that brings stressful things to be a mynd vandal
It's you not knowing how to deal with things positively yeah you're the one that

don't know how to handle
The pitfalls of life when they are evident and come about
That's why you're losing the battle a little simple one round bout
You won't take a new route I guess maybe stupidity or maybe cause you scary
The reason I'm telling you all this is because of the life and death of Mary
You see she had this way about her, which didn't allow all this pain in this world to overcome her mynd and take her to a planet of hate
And seems like it has passed on to one of the people that was able to create
And that's me of course who is trying to get you from being so very very wary
Don't hate me for being born and giving you this it's not because of me it's because of my Mary

Because of her I was born to tell you all this love she made me physically and by the way that I handled things. Thank you Mary Ju I love you. Druce.

Thank you with love, something cute from and for my Mary

Love Druce

The Mastel
Copyright Mastel 2002

Dear Everybody
Dear Everybody,

This is a letter to everybody who thinks that I am stupid for always thinking about my Mary or death. I think you should think about it too. You need to wonder when its going to be your time to go and if God will accept what type of life that you were found living. Do you curse? Do you think God likes to hear that? Do you have sex before you are married? Do you think God likes to see that? Do you have sex with other men or other women while you're married? Do you withhold sex from your spouse, which would make him or her lust after others that they are not to have? Do you drink alcoholic drinks which leads to drunkenness or do you smoke or take anything that is not naturally made by God for your body? Do you read your bible and try to learn more about God and a better way of life? If you answered yes to any of these questions except the last one, then you really should think about Mary and not just her but that the very thing that has taken her from me, death, is going to happen to you. What's going to happen when you get trapped in the world of the non-living? Do you think that you can just shake death off and just wake up and be living again? I wish it was that easy myself but its not. When my Mary was murdered by the facility where she was supposed to be receiving care, she was competent and very coherent, able to understand and talk to you in a normal conversation. She was not just a old and senile person who couldn't comprehend, but she was alive, and I've got to say that when she was dying she didn't even see it coming. I didn't even see it coming. We thought she had a little while longer to be here, but she didn't. She was bleeding because of sores and the nurses had given her the wrong medicine which forced her more into the coma, it just was so miserable for her to have to go through that, but the point of my story is just this. While she had a few days to prepare for God and the day of reckoning, you have more than that right now. What are you doing with all this good time that God has given to you? How are you living right now? Do you know what's going to happen to you or your family members today or later on today or tomorrow or whenever? That's why it's so important that you look at death in a very beautiful way. Not sad or in fear, but in the beautiful way that God wants you to look at it. You should want to die to be able to see your long gone ones. You should want to die most of all so that you will be able to see your true creator, your maker and my maker, our real daddy, our father in heaven, our God, the one who's gonna show you all the missing love and understanding that no one here could give you. He will hear you when no one else will. He will be compassionate when no one else will. He won't be mean to you or anyone that you care about, because he cares about you and them too, so think about death and how you can improve your life before you're trapped in the world of the non-living and have no place to go when you leave this apartment.

Love truly,

Druce

P.S. I didn't forget your poem.

Leaving My Apartment

Every time I have to move it seems kinda sad
Sometimes I don't want to but sometimes I'm glad
The sometimes I don't want to is because I have found me some friends or family that are nice
The sometimes that I was glad was because those people in that complex were mean with hatred and cold as ice
But nevertheless I have to move so I gotta get everything prepared and ready
Because if I don't then my place of residence won't be real or steady
I'll be struggling to survive and I probably won't make it at all
Not preparing to leave an apartment will confirm a very hard fall
I'll have no place to call home because I didn't consider to plan ahead
And that's what it'll be like if you don't prepare before you're dead
You see this body that we're in is just an apartment with a short lease to live
So while you're in it prepare for your next and new home without the negatives
All the negatives that hold you back from preparing for your next home are already known
So fix them while God gave you a chance before your time is all gone
Your lease will be up soon and you'll be next to follow the steps of my Mary
Remember these words of Druce as you take me to the cemetery

From Druce by Druce for Everyone listening

The Mastel
Copyright Mastel 2002

Realizing Death

Every time I wake up I realize that I don't have very much time left
And every time I tell somebody about it they get mad because they hate that I talk about death
Who's to say that death is wrong, I mean I do believe that it is suppose to happen to every person that exist
We all are like vapors like the bible says that evaporate into time like a mist
I'm not sad about the situation so whenever you hear me talk about it don't get mad at me and talk all crazy
I guess I just don't want to let my consciousness about life just go on all lazy
I think about it I guess because I've experienced death recently through Unk Junior and my momma Mary
And they made it a whole lot easier for me to look forward to my time in the cemetery
Because I saw them leave gracefully regardless if it was to be or if it was murder in the worst degree
I knew he had cancer but from that certain Atlanta health center it was pure hurt to me
How could you kill without knowing how that would make me feel
I never thought it could happen to me but you sick people proved to me that it was real
I came by there the day before you started your evil plot against human life
And I asked you….. I begged you….. not to stab us with that poisonous knife
You did anyway and it seems like whenever I think about my Mary I think about what you evil people did
Because she told me that day that you were going to do it and it was because I asked you to let her live
I asked you desperately to remember how you would feel cause I knew that when you did it that I wasn't going to be able to take it
You did it anyway killed my heart and God made me write the poem that was entitled Hatred
You prompted a series of letters and poems that makes me seem kinda wacko and twisted in the head
The poem No More was right there at the funeral written stroftly for the dead
You made me weak and made me feel like grabbing my knuckles and bawling up my fist
But I wasn't allowed to do so because there is a God that lives that makes all vengeance exist

If you get a chance to review my work you'll probably see some of yourself in my poetic mynd reflection
And if it moves you enough I hope that you have an emotional God prompted concession
A concession of compassion for the love that was here that loved me and her family and that by you got up and left
I thank you cruel people for helping me learn the good in realizing death

Thank you to the Imperial caregivers

The Mastel
Copyright Mastel 2002

Chapter 2...

When I see the light

Me and My Black Suit

There was once upon a time I looked good in my black suit
But the wearing of it so frequently doesn't feel too cute
Murders over here cancers over there death is everywhere
Sometimes I wonder in this planet who really cares
Cause death is all around me seems too too numeral
Every time I turn around my black suit and a funeral
When will this black suit ever get a chance to rest?
Maybe when I leave myself in the presence of death
But until that day I guess I'll just have to sit and wait
And try not to let my feelings of death turn into hate
God told me this was supposed to happen in the beginning
And he told me I could meet him and them if I'd stop sinning
So I'll try my best to see if I can leave things minuet
Lord forgive me for crying me, me and my black suit

Death!!!
For Gloria and others
BY D. ROUZAN A.K.A. THE MASTEL

COPYRIGHT MASTEL 2002

Judgment Day pt 1

God forgive me please cause I'm doin sinz that I don't wanna
I know if I don't study right then I'm a be a gonna
Not to the essence a place of where my presence iz destined
To hell and beyond and never see effervescence
Check out tha story yo as I drop a jewel tha lesson
About mankind tha start a tyme and all tha blessinz
1st thing 1st goin to tha revelations verse
What happens to tha body when ya 1st leavin tha hurst
Okay it waz appointed to every man in this life to die
Don't ask me why just go and tell your moms don't cry
Then comes tha judgment when God's tyme to judge tha spirit
Tha knowledge hear it fear it and simply step near it
He judges tha tyme whether you waz good or waz bad
Remember doin all tha sinz and all tha fun that cha had
Lyin gambling hustling and all tha shots you waz bussinin
You knew it waz wrong still ya went ahead and did it anyway
Knowin tha Lord God was gonna have him a judgment day
But back cipher spinnin to the design once again
Tha God of heaven simply judges you all your sinz
And if you repented and really meant it on tha real
Tha God considers inside of maybe makin you a deal
But if you didn't repent and wasn't even baptized
That's when you finally realize on you it waz tha disguise
Sun gets strucked word up and now ya ran outta luck
No one can help you so in hell you gets stuck

Mentally Mastel
Copyright Mastel 2002

What is it do you really want in Life?

Question, what is it you really want in life? What plans or goals have you made for yourself or if you have a family? Do you include God in the picture frame of your mind or how do you think of God? Seems like every answer I get for that question is "I love God, I know what he did for me, he's the greatest. But do you really? Do you really love him and know all he did for you besides Jesus dying? He has given you more than you are awarding him for. I'm going to give you some instances of how the love of God is overlooked probably by you and you probably know it and don't care, then again you probably don't even know and are too stubborn to yourself and God to give up enough time to find out, but listen to this. God gave a certain woman that had no understanding of how strong the spirit of God was, a more so spiritual man as a husband. Now the man wasn't that bad of a man and he was more so a spiritual man but just as every man he had some faults. Now these faults could have been corrected if she was willing to help him when he cried out for help, but Satan decided to interrupt the upright plans of this man's household through his wife's confused and spiritually undeveloped mind. He gave thoughts of deception to his wife's mind to make her believe that God's way of living and dealing with things or problems was not the right way out. I don't want to take your mind off the focus of the primary question, but stay with me, it's coming. Now according to faith and scripture God has consistently told us humans to give our troubles to him and that he will take care of them. It is proven beyond fact that everyone has some fear of committing to God, so the first thing that seems easy to do is to make excuses of why you can't so that you can force yourself to believe you have a reason not to. Sometimes the excuses are different and continue to follow one another unless something is said to make the excuses collapse. These excuses are created by a combination of fear of what might happen (lack of experience for some) and the continuing lack of daily study for learning better. The woman always had one of these excuses of why she couldn't believe, study, serve, worship, and fellowship at God's place of worship. This was the point that the man tried to tell his wife, but self-examination was not a thought for the woman. She would not listen to anything that the man suggested, instead, she discouraged the man from being a better Christian and tried to encourage him to become a better sinner. She act as if she couldn't see that what the man was trying to was to bring them closer to God. She made light of everything and told him that he was just making an excuse of why he won't be a certain way that she wanted him *to be. Now don't get me wrong, everything sinful that the man did was his own fault and went against his own individual slate with God, and he knew this. He knew that if he did not get it right and stay right that his destination was hell, but the inspiration from his wife was not positive inspiration toward a godly behavior. Her words of inspiration would become degrading to her husband provoking him to anger and sin. She would call him stupid and told him that his faith in God was not serious and that him fellowshipping with the spiritual brethren a bad thing. She said that he was going to church to impress people and not God. Who made her the judge? And how far do you think you can get without God or godly people to help encourage you? I tell you that this woman wrecked her marriage because of the constant negativity that she was filled with that was a result of non-knowledge, no understanding, and no study of God's words. I talked to her about it and told her the story about the woman who had a very unspiritual husband (non-Christian) ,but she wanted her husband to be a Christian man and the other woman who was sinful, had a Christian man ,but encouraged wrongness to God. The first woman was raised in church by her parents. She had problems with the man disrespecting her by being very profane to her. He also beat her and loved to get drunk, smoke, and be involved with other women but she still loved him and tried to encourage him to become godly. So I asked her the question "How did you hook up with him?"? Her reply was "I thought that I wanted a thug at first but I have found out that that was not what I really wanted". "I was very naïve and not focused on what God wanted". "It's a lot of women that would just kill for a half way descent man these days and I'm one of them". "I guess I have to keep on praying and maybe it'll work out". When she was done talking, I told her about the woman who had the Christian type man that she was talking about and that this particular woman would not involve herself with any of the positive things that this man had for them. Instead, she discouraged his ideas and would not accept anything that he felt. The question then was, were you that woman? Were you that woman at one point that discouraged her husband to the point that he went sour? Were you the one at one time that when a good man was given to you you showed your displease ness by all of the degrading and negativity? If so, you were blessed with a good spouse, but it was you that ruined him and it's going to take you to sit down first with God (study) then with your husband and try to encourage and inspire him with a better wife presentation than you did before. Are you able to acknowledge you at fault in this situation? If you are then you can stop it now. You can stop it now by not continuing to degrade your husband. You can stop it by not condemning his ideas that he has about yall and the fellowshipping with other members of the church. Fellowshipping will only encourage and inspire the two of you to grow stronger spiritually* as well as with the love that you have for each other. He has tried to get you involved with the church and church functions, don't deny or forsake that. It is very detrimental for you both. And stop making excuses of why you can't and start making excuses of why you can. This type of negative influence does not inspire a man to be close to you or God. Take a close look at yourself and ask yourself "WHAT DO I REALLY WANT IN THIS LIFE? Do I want a life with God and a godly man to guide me and our kids to glory or do I want to know what my family and friends think for me and him? Do I want to be like the woman in the story and have home grown thug that I know will end up in the grave or a prison? Do I want God for my kids or do I want them fatherless? WHAT DO YOU WANT? Stop all this sinful gossip and sinful inspiration and provocation!! Become a woman that stands for God, you kids, your husband, and yourself. Get some knowledge while you have a chance, because there is no telling how long that good man is going to allow you to tear up his household with your unspiritual inspiration. There's no telling how long God's gonna go for it. He might take him from you if he sees you abusing the blessing that he gave you. Be a Christian while you can and have this opportunity to. There are a lot of people that don't have this opportunity that you have now. They probably had it, but look at them now. Get some knowledge!!!! Read your bible. So many people are like the woman in the story and wish that they could see to read the bible and learn life. What are you doing with your eyesight? Letting it go to waste? Stop being so wasteful with your blessings!! You have some great blessings, don't take them for granted, cause God giveth and God taketh, especially when you are not doing right with it. What's your choice heaven....or is it hell? ....Please choose right from wrong. I love you and I want you to take some time and love yourself. Thanks!!

D. Rouzan

THE MASTEL
Copyright Mastel 2002

Hatred

Hatred. So many people wonder where it comes from. Some wonder if it comes from God and some wonder if it comes from Satan, but nevertheless, hatred is described as intense animosity or hostility or a strong feeling of displeasure. My interpretation of hatred is having an extreme feeling of dislike from one being to another. Most of the time in existence, hatred is taught. Other times hatred is provoked by one person's selfishness about another person's feelings, perceptions, or outlook on a situation. I witnessed an act of hatred today and it made me think about why do we as individuals receive this….this hatred from others. Well as I said earlier sometimes hatred is taught and sometimes it's provoked. I looked at how the God of heaven and earth talked to us as creatures of his image and love and one very strong piece of advice that I boldly remember was how he told us to treat one another like we would want to be treated. I looked at how sometimes when hatred is engaged on us, we wonder….why was that hatred invoked on me? Have you ever thought about that there was time that you probably invoked hatred on somebody else, for whatever reason? Did you ever look at yourself to see if you were hating someone right now? What about thinking if this could be payback for how you hated someone in your past? Well here's a poem that should describe it all:

Hatred

Hatred is a feeling of dislike that is taught from man to man
It is something that is shown to do from one land to another land
What land do you hate and do you hate them that you want them to burn
I ask that question because one day its goin to be your turn
Your turn to be on the receiving end of the ugliest time wasted
the time of animosity for no reason at all the time for you to receive hatred
How bad do you hate me because there is a God and its going to be ten times your worst
Because you hated me for no reason at all or you were the one that hated first
It's a proven fact that hatred is taught and that it's not an natural instinct
You shouldn't get mad when it comes back to you because you were warned to think
Think about the hatred you had to a person because of a thing of color
When all the time you hated me not knowing that I was you brother
No matter how you look at it all hatred is considered sin
Unless your hatred is to sin itself, please let me begin
To heal your mynd from that poison before your building gets hit, crumbles, and fall
Still don't remember the time when you didn't want love for all
All is all and you can stop it by really trading your life in to God and truly stop disliking others
For if you hate them for being born, then you soon, you or your kids will be hated by another
Rather it's through you or through the very love of your life
If you have hatred in your heart, it most definitely will be sliced with the hatred knife
The very knife that exist negatively down in the depths of your heart
You live by the sword, you die by the sword now how was that thinking smart
Don't even think about questioning why God did this or that I must retaliate for this hate
Cause all you're going to do is prove the theory true that to acquire hatred you must educate
You've been educating hatred within your society and culture for such a long time
What's wrong right now with you changing your mynd
Whether you learn it or if it is provoked on you, it's solely on you to decide to take it
Please!!!, listen to God if not me and run hard away from your hatred

BY GOD AND D. ROUZAN

THE MASTEL
COPYRIGHT MASTEL

Can't Miss Every Bump in Tha Road

With everyday of life comes so many episodes
A parallel to a day in life I consider as a road
A road that is paved before you even drive down that street
But no road is perfect and all candy isn't sweet
I traveled a particular day thinking that things were okay
Not knowing which imperfections were going to be in my way
I knew to be concerned cause life has no maps of destinies
And I know that all the tyme one doesn't have all the recipes
Recipes to surpass trouble when it comes in your direction
The best recipe for that is preparation or get some protection
No matter what preparing you do though nothing is ever perfect
Like the soul of a man when he internally searches it
There's always going to be a crack, a crook, and maybe even a stain
But you've got to understand that there's no gain without pain
There's no glory without struggles no success without trials
No getting into heaven without living a bit of whiles
And whenever problems come try your best to smile and not to explode
And remember this little phrase cause you can't miss all the bumps in the road

The Mastel
Copyright Mastel 2002

Lil Black Horner

Lil black horner
Sat on a corner eating some American pie
He tried to get a job
The others made it hard and made a way for the black man to die
He tried to fight back
But the law wasn't black and found out that he was in prison
Too much liquor indeed
Along with the weed which crippled his mynd's vision
He sees no more
But loving a whore that holds his God's spirit for a ransom
She cut his <u>hair</u>
His life turned bare here we are now a new black Samson
I pray by day
That maybe some day he will re-gain his entire strength
And maybe <u>Delilah</u>
Will kill her fire and help him to grow the whole length
To reach the goal
To save his soul if not us blacks are some goners
Please Dear God
Hear my sob about me the lil black horner

The Mastel
Copyright Mastel 2002

When its my time...

When its my time I wonder will I die in pain
Similar to 2pac or my Mary Julia slain
Will it be like Malcolm X and or Martin Luther King
Still trying to get these white people to let freedom ring

When it's my time will it be with a violent accident
Will I have reached my goals in life am I heaven sent
To give these humans the paths to God's righteousness
Will I die with a heart full of fear or full of fighteousness

When it's my time will I see myself go slowly with cancer
Will I finally be able to understand the white man's answer
To the question of why in this life I had to struggle harder
Than all the white kids did and even to be myself a father

When it's my time will you really and truly miss me
Will you kiss me or burn harder feeling guilty
For hating me and my kids for no reason at all
Will you then begin to tear down your ignorant wall

When it's my time will my blood pressure be the cause
Of the stroke that I had and then fell on all fours
Begging you to help thinking you were my sister or my brother
When all the time you were disguised as a winter whiter hearted other

When it's my time will you tell my kids that I loved them a lot
No matter how many times that other people forgot
To love them the same as if they were always me equal
When it is my time God forgive me and these uncompassionate people

When it's my time...
Copyright Mastel 2002

My Sinz

I wonder why is it every day I have death on my mynd
Is it soon to end my stay or is it almost about my time
Or is it God calling me saying come away from those streets
I need you my son to make my words live so complete
Follow your brother's footsteps as well as your earthly father
And soon you will see these death demons stop trying to bother
Your soul and your mynd giving you visions of a painful fatality
Stop being so rough and make my mentality become your reality
Cause truly in the end if you at least tried to fight sin
Your troubles will be over and forgiven and I will receive and let you in

Forgive my sinz
The Mastel

The Little Lost Black Sheep

The little lost black sheep
Finding God's commandment hard to keep
He strayed away forgot about judgment day and was destined in hell to weep
When will you change the shepherd's helper would say
Before our father has his judgment's day
Do you want to forever in torment stay
In the fiery pits where all the demons lay
The little black sheep had no reply
When it looked at itself it would just sigh and cry
Thinking of how close it and the shepherd use to fly
Trying to remember how the shepherd showed it how to die
I am to die with God's grace
When its time for me to leave this place
I pray to the father this very second to wipe the tears from my face
And make me like Samson to be strong once then and then again
Because my heart has grown cloudy completely stained with sin
I can't feel my life tomorrow
All I feel is some future sorrow
Please Dear God help me with beautiful life that I have borrowed
I don't want to do wrong anymore all I want to do now is rest in peace and sleep
Please God forgive me your little lost black sheep

The Mastel
Copyright Mastel 2002

Reflections

Reflections are images that are matched by the same force of energy
Whenever someone presents themselves as enemy that makes me unfriendly
Reflections of you is what makes me become what it is that I am
When you reflect tensions of negativity it makes me not even do what I can
Reflections of love, kindness, spirituality, goodness, and God's compassion
Allows me to be filled with tenderness and a humbleness for an everlasting
Reflections of hope allows me to believe in things that I would never believe
But reflection of some lies would probably make me untruthful and want to deceive
If you reflected hatred, tell me, what could one possibly expect
Could they expect love, kindness, compassion, or even receive good respect
If I want someone to respect me I have to give it if I want good respect
Cause if not then how I respect myself is how others will look and reflect
Like a cursed mirror hanging, right in the middle of my bedroom wall
If I present myself in front of that mirror fancy, then I am the fairest of all
If I present myself as ugly, mean, nasty; run get that mirror some protections
Cause I have hurt it and myself with these destructive reflections
If I reflect hate for color or with friendship how can that be seen as good
Cause if I was the outsider I would see villainous people I know I would
Someone reflecting a plot of evil is what my thoughts would behold
So I began to reflect some counter negative plots that dwell in the evil half of my soul
You want some good reflections then reflect some love, compassion, and positivity
Cause if not you could reflect some hateful ways some extreme negativity
I myself try to reflect truth, justice, and realness while there are still so many deceptions
What do you illuminate, what do others see inside of your reflections

The Mastel
Copyright Mastel 2003

Support for Married Folks

Support my mynd by keeping God on it
Support my body by making love to it with no conditions
Support my soul by baptizing Christ in your heart with me
Support my goals by looking to a future of godliness
Support my focus by inspiring positive energy
Support my love for you through your reflections
Support us with compassion for God's creations of life
Support us with spiritual awareness of each other
Support my thoughts by at least listening to them
Support my smile by smiling yourself
Support spirituality by telling me and others who don't know
Support righteousness instead of darkness
Support my children by loving them as I do
Support my culture by living in it with me
Support my humility by being humble yourself
Support my problems without being against me
Support peace by not being for hatred
Support our faults by suggesting a solution
Support our existence with the rest of our life
Support me lover in the similitude as husband and wife

Support our marriage

The Mastel
Copyright Mastel 2003

Support for Open Minded Mankind

Support my mynd by keeping God on it
Support my soul by baptizing Christ in your heart with me
Support my goals by looking to a future of godliness
Support my focus by inspiring positive energy
Support my love for you through your reflections
Support us with compassion for God's creations of life
Support us with spiritual awareness of each other
Support my thoughts by at least listening to them
Support my smile by smiling yourself
Support spirituality by telling me and others who don't know
Support righteousness instead of darkness
Support my children by loving them as I do
Support my culture by living in it with me
Support my humility by being humble yourself
Support my problems without being against me
Support peace by not being for hatred
Support our faults by suggesting a solution
Support my race by not looking at my color
Support yourself by letting me be your sister or your brother

Support us.

The Mastel
Copyright Mastel 2003

Free (to heaven)

One of these days I gonna really be who I am
I'm gonna really be me
No more locked inside of being something that I'm not
I can be honest and free
Free to the skies
Free to God with the truth and no lies
I can be free like the before Adam without wearin a disguise
Free from prison
Inside of a government's mynd
With niggaz living like the enemy
Free from people that hate me
And those that fake love me and pretend to me
Free from all sin
All prejudice
And hatred whatever the form of attack
Free from bill collectors and problems
Free from being considered colored or black
Free from color at all
And all stressful extremities that be
I thank God and sweet Jesus
Cause through death I can finally and truly be free

The Mastel
Copyright Mastel 2003

The Rare Jewel

So prepared never scared the mynd frame is rared
Like a jewel speak to fools while leaving em mad clues
I twist a mynd's kiss so conspicuous
But still my fate create results of hate
The mynd shine design becomes tha mynd valentine
But still its so real in the streets it gets ill
No change rearrange governmental so strange
Oppose black foes see the heart it dosed close
The set neglect text respect my hang necks
The hang man thang man the kill what up flex
The rhyme time prime time please just find time
Envision decision change hate conditions
From black to white the one sided iz not right
I still shine bright like the sun through the nite
With the spark ness regardless the godless darkness
They dead in the head without trustin the read

The Mastel
Copyright Mastel 2003

One Try...

One try for you to receive
One try for you to believe
That it is true love that I want to achieve
When will you open your heart
As well as your body and soul
Receive me as your husband(lover)
That's been my God given goal
All I wanna do is love you
Till the black day that I die
I could shine through the darkness
Real love with one try

The Mastel
Copyright Mastel 2003

One Wife...

One wife is all that a black Samson like me needs
That's if she wants to be that one true Sarah indeed
With being that one there's little that she must read
And that's what type of food it takes for his need to feed
Its your mynd with God and then your body in passion
With a soul of receiving my true love everlasting
No rejections cause of rules, or conditions to be given
So that in harmony we can easily be living
Being able to admit when she may possibly be wrong
And know without friends how to sing our love's song
I say all this to say that God gave me only one life
All I need in this one world, one me, is the compassionate one wife

The Mastel
Copyright Mastel 2003

Lookin Through Shaded Windows

Lookin through shaded windows you can never see light
The only thing that you see is the darkness of plight
Hatred ignorance selfishness no kinda love at all
You standin up right now but you're beginning to fall
Eventually crawl from not letting the light in
To guide you away from evil ways of men and women
Who pretend to lead you with these negative influences
Look at love and its opposition what hatred induces
Is a realm of negativity bothering your inner spirit see
No light too long begins to burden your mentalities
Blyndness becomes the only thing your eyes can focus
Sometimes so painful you wish for more than hocus-pocus
God iz here speakin to you through me so listen
Your friendz may hate you but rewards come being a Christian
Look for true light or your life's corrupt or abrupt
Open up your blynds for loving times and keep the shades up

The Mastel
Copyright Mastel 2003

The analogy of this poem is to get mankind to open up their senses to accept positive inspirations and influences instead of viewing life negatively, critically, and through the souls of those that are experiencing difficult times without God as their lean on.

Thank you.

Never saw it Comin (death)

If today was your last day would you begin to start runnin
Toward the crown of God if you had a chance to see it comin
This inspiration comes from the Great Masterful Lord of the sky
To get you thinking about an early death before opportunity passes you by
Opportunity to fix your life when you thought it was just gas or chest pains
You thought it was just a hospital visit but now only your family still remains
To be there for the news to hear the struggling words the doctor and God have said
Instead of saying you're going to be okay they've pronounced your obituary to be read
Oh you thought I was gonna say dead but that's already an established fact
Once you take that walk with the death angel ain't gone be no turning back
Thinkin God's wordz were slack you were warned to pay close attention
I wonder if you had a chance to make it in or is there an honorable mentioned
Or maybe it was a fall that you thought the pain would shortly go away
Not knowing that that particular fall was the beginning of your ending day
The day that you and death finally got a chance to make that unbridled love
You became the hand in time and death fitted you perfectly unlike an O.J. glove
Now it could've been an accident like a car crash or one of life's fatal fates
There's only one that created the beginning and it's the ending he also creates
Gunshot blast to the head or to the chest without protection of a bulletproof vest
Or maybe you were probably the ones who got murdered to kill nursing home stress
Whatever the situation I urge you strongly to be spiritual cause out of time you are runnin
And don't be like a lot of people that we both knew and loved that never saw it comin

See it comin…

The Mastel
Copyright Mastel 2003

They Judge Me before They Know Me

They judge me before they know me
Like pharaoh did God's glory
I don't know why in life I guess its ignorant mandatory
For mankind to place hatred
Worst time wasted
But judging their own faults it's hard for them to face it
Yet instill hatred pains me
These accusations train me
To break every barrier they use against me to chain me
Women, color, stupid people
Screamin lies that we equal
Black women and men treat one another like we just fecal
No love or concern with me
Heart actin black n shifty
Made my soul full of clouds and my spirit of mynd misty
Accused like I'm Black Jesus
Well here's the fact thesis
None of your antagonism here creates bad features
However you judge me believe you gon be judge too
So watch how you judge me that's how God's gon judge you
Judgin me harshly God's gonna judge you harshly
Judgin with friends you get your life judged partially
In the end don't pretend to intend to listen
Cause God'll judge you right if you did live like a Christian
I'm on a mission with my heart full of ambition
I forgot to mention shut your mouth up and pay attention
To this mynd shyne valentine God filled Mastamynd
Get your soul intertwine with my spiritual line the sign
For you to learn grow earn make your life's right turn
Wisdom gets to know me before a dummy's discern return
To the title of this entire story
Don't judge me before you know me

The Mastel
Copyright Mastel 2003

As I look Into My Soul...

As I look into my soul I can see me infinite as space
7 different mynds in the soul take me to a 7 different place
Mynd #1 has God overshining the light of the sun
While mynd #2 is constantly thinking about nothing good to do
Mynd #3 loves to love all eternally
While mynd #4 looks at faith and closes the door
Mynd #5 makes me wanna survive and stay alive
While mynd #6 makes me wanna hurry to the 6-foot ditch
Mynd #7 has me staying strong to make it into heaven
While the rest of my soul thanks the Lord for this lesson

Mastel
Copyright Mastel 2003

Don't Criticize before You Open Your Eyes

I'm sorry if this poem doesn't rhyme all the way through cause it wasn't meant for that. It was expressly meant for the encouraging and nourishing of your mynd, so please follow with an open mynd. Thanks.

Don't criticize before you open your eyes
Just cause you don't see the sun/son right now
Doesn't mean it won't rise
Just cause you don't see me as pretty as you right now
Doesn't mean that God's not going to show me how
To believe in his glory, his strength, his Lord's mercy
Criticism too early made you wanna hurt and curse me
Before you even got a chance to see who tha black I waz
I probably was your brother or your nearby family cuz
Why ya criticizin me and don't even know who I be
Is cause I ain't part of tha same family color of tree
Is it because you like to judge books by the looks of their cover
Are you that different person that constantly misjudges their lover
Are you that one that clings hard to your false perception
With your eyes closed against me seeing the wrong direction
When all the time your wasting time it has wings and just flies
Look at me with you mental eyes before you begin to criticize

Don't criticize before you open your eyes the storm is coming
So you'd better start running cause the Lord is coming
The rain and the hell will you be frail or prevail
Or be subjected to fail criticizin my sail
God be with us as we make our humane mistakes
And forgive those who leap before lookin forward for hates
I'm erecting my life to give my soul to Christ
Look both ways crossing the street was tha old advice
So I do come through with the new to be true
Realize what I advise open mynds and get a clue
Before you get caught up with thinkin my life lies
Please don't criticize before you open your eyes

The Mastel
Copyright Mastel 2003

Give God the Praise

Give God the Praise
For forgiving me of this phase
Lord I wanna change my ways
But my mynd it goes astrays
Seems like I'm stays up in a daze
Interference when I prays
People close they always plays
This life is like a maze
When will I get to the end
Cause my folk they just pretend
Have hatred unlike a friend
Insteadily I must depend
On the one that gave me life
Not the one that gave me strife
Cut me many times with the knife
If I am Samson then who's my wife
Give God the praise
For not one but all the 7 days
Wanna go to heaven never blaze
Continue to give God the praise

The Mastel
Copyright Mastel 2003

Gratification with No gratitude

Gratification with no gratitude
Is like love with an attitude
Don't mean to be rude but I gotta job to do
To explain to masses that means you the people
That if God or anybody's good thank them equal
Cause if not then maybe your blessings will begin to change
Then you're angry cause everybody's acting strange
It ain't everybody its you why won't you see
Look both ways before you cross the street
Look your way to see the ignorance that you caused
Seeing yourself through yourself helps you fix the flaws
Then you can be grateful to people without the question
Did I thank God today counting all my blessings
Did I thank God for even giving things that's small
Did I think about no God how I almost could've fall
Anyway forgive me selves for being so vainly crude
And for your gratification here's my gratitude

The Mastel
Copyright Mastel 2003

Have Hatred

Have hatred since that's how you want your time wasted
No love to replace it I guess yall stuck up in that matrix
(Have hatred) Still basic when it comes to trivial type things
Black women don't wanna be queens and they men to be kings
Kings don't wanna be kings but become pimps and weed supporters
Support bad habits of drinking not support the sons and daughters
Reasons why they run to pimpin smokin weed and liquor drinking
Has me searching to find the major reasons so I sit back thinkin
Bout my own experiences of all the false appearances
That women gave to men and me made life delirious
How they start beefs not knowing they passin hatred in the action
2 over 1 1 over 2 the reciprocation of the fraction
Basically a mirror image a reflection if I may
And if the image is undesirable how can a good man stay
If you tear him down and knowing that he's already down
You can't build him up unless you've tried to heal him up fill him up
With love through support of graceful words not words of hate
That's how you begin to inspire positive to go through your mate
He already knows that there's a complication with a situation
But kickin him while he's down won't help that's called aggravation
If you failed or made a mistake on something on your part
Would you want your mate to push you away or to back you with his heart
You don't do, so the wrong things come and its part cause yall stress it
To makin a black Samson re-occur and choose the wrong exit
I ask you women no I'm begging you black women please
Look into your soul to find to cure of the hatred disease
So you don't pass it on like a cold or the worst tyme wasted
Have vision as I stated re-arrange a change and oppose having hatred

Mastel
Copyright The Mastel 2003

He Died Trying

He died trying to get ignorant people to open and see the light
He died trying to make everything become focused and in God's sight
He died trying to make everybody live with love happily
He died because too many people was bussing shots at me
He died because of all the hatred that men possessed within their hearts
He died because of no support from his wife, which tore him <u>entirely</u> apart
He died trying to get both of them to understand
That positive focus is better than hatred from woman to her husbandman
He died trying to be truthful against mankind and evil women's darkness
He died trying to make peace live in the heart of all the godless
He died trying to show others that love always conquers over its enemy hatred
And he died trying to teach that love or hatred is whatever you want to make it
You can make love become hate by losing sight of the rules for love
You can learn hatred from the wrong examples that you keep on thinking of
You can turn hatred into love being true to yourself then others without lying
These are just a few things he couldn't give you alive but he did die trying

The Mastel
Copyright Mastel 2003

Chapter 3...
What do you look for during and after the storm?

All of my Blessings...

Love Love

From all the wrong that I do to all the right that I know
Please dear father forgive me move the weed so I can grow
Grow into an Angel with the biggest wings to fly
High above Satan cause all he wants is me to die
He is full of loving hatred and he passes it all around
Lord knows I've seen so much hatred why do they want to see me down
Why in my own house must I live like Paul or Jesus
And why do these people for hatred try to give me these hatred diseases
Want me to hate them cause they are so stained with hatred
I know nothing can come of it cause hatred is tyme wasted
Tyme that could a been spent with goodness from up above
Make us humans hate hatred and learn to love love

Mastel
Copyright Mastel 2003

Mistakes

We all make mistakes some big ones some small
But admitting your wrong faults is what makes you stand tall
Especially if someone close tried to tell you ahead of time
This ain't a poem sayin I told you so but to help you clear up yo mynd
The stuff that I'm sayin now consider it real as all hell
And expect more promising inspirations from the mynd of the Mastel
A snake is always slicker than a real friend's hair grease
No matter what form it comes in it will never mean you peace
Whether it's the bottle or a decision a snake is always a snake
And not knowing it at all you could be the form the snake will take
And when you are that form you can be harmful to self and to others
You wind up with a domino effect affecting not just you but your team full of brothers
Mothers sisters your children that makes you are the snake of all the snakes
Learn from and correct yourself I try not to make my same mistakes

For you baby boy you know who you are…

The Mastel
Copyright Mastel 2003

Never Hard to Deal with God

Man I'm lookin at myself and I see my past has been kinda rough
But seeing that I'm still here says God made me tough enough
To endure hatred from white people as well as some of the blax
To seeing that things here won't change and these are just the facts
The facts that concern me though are prevalent not the same kinda odd
It may be hard to deal with these crazy people but it's never hard to deal with God

Mastel
Copyright Mastel 2003

Show Me Love

I use to know love seems like so many lifetimes ago
That if love from that special girl would come right now I wouldn't even know
If she meant what she said and if she said it from her heart
Would she really love for us to be together or would she love for us to be apart
While my mynd's traveling I'm lookin for that perfect thought to catch
An imagination of love for me and my children of me to match
Someone that would have that different love from all others she was set apart
Love so true and odd a queen that wears the crown of God
Someone smart that embraced the values of the living God's words of the bible
Someone far from Delilah that used Sarah has her American Idol
Someone special that whenever needed she would give real support and a loving shove
This done turn into a prayer please Lord send them to show me love

Love Mastel
Copyright Mastel 2003

The Cancer Patient

When I first met you you seemed as if you had love for me
You seemed as if you had love for me and a branch of my tree
You alluded my eye to make me believe that you were what was best for me
Now all I see is a broken rainbow with more severe storms to be
I thought you were the answer but now you've seem to become the question
Why couldn't you know how to love basically and be able to count us in all your blessings
Hatred was born in your heart and it is about to spread badly like some deadly cancer
You said you wanted me to be your everything your answer and your love romancer
I did that as a dancer until my love dance became same ol to your sharp immaturity
I gave you all of me at once to show you that I had that bold strong security
You received me at first but quickly sent our love to the hurst
And told me that all your youthful eyes did see was that love was a curse
A curse for loneliness with just you and my child and my presence dead
Is that what was shown to your young mynd as a young woman to be bred
Excuse me for interrupting because that is the wrong way to suppose
That marriage was all about accusal and schemes for us to constantly throw blows
To use a person of lifetime for your own self righteousness and your own personal gain
Are you ready to look at yourself and see how you're creating all of your own pain
Many of times have I tried to cure your hatred for me but like cancer it continues to spread
I guess just like a cancer patient you won't stop your hatred until I'm all the way dead
You take the wrong medicine from your associates that know nothing about us or real love
I mean if they did they wouldn't growl about it they would just give the perfect example of
They wouldn't converse of negativity like those uncertified nurses always do
They would tell you truthfully that way you can see how the success of our love grew
If you take a closer look you wouldn't say that I'm nothing and that you've always had to carry me
Because I always did nice things with or without money for you and your family

every since I said marry me
I sacrificed my life really to be yours and just yours only forever
You tell me you did the same thing but every other week your statement is whatever
I sacrificed my mynd by having you on it throughout your good times and life threatening surgeries
And I can't even count or remember the so many times that I was the doctor for some of your emergencies
I sacrificed my child for you because you felt some jealousy and you thought you were too crowdy
And even though you didn't ask me directly I sacrificed my God, which made me become sinful and too rowdy
I eventually sacrificed my name and credit so that your name and credit wouldn't be considered negligent
And even though you won't acknowledge it I still voted for you to be my queenly president
I sacrificed my car to walk with your ideal that was supposed to advance both of us
I soon after lost my job and for months had to walk with my head down to cry out dust
I almost sacrificed my freedom just to try to make you happy content and satisfied
And I proceeded on to get advancement to make us rise higher and extremely qualified
I've done all that I can to do good but like the cancerous I guess I just gotta face it
The doctor said there's nothing more we can do because hatred has made you the cancer patient

The Mastel
Copyright Mastel 2003

The Special One

Your spirit is like a rainbow...
Cause all my life I've had a storm...
So many times I've been hated on...
And like a ship, beat, wrecked, and torn...
Every since I boarded this ship...
I've been mistreated just like a slave...
And through all of the stormy weather...
God gave me courage and kept me brave...
The storm lasted all of the night...
I thought I wasn't gonna ever see the sun/son...
Lost everything on the ship...
Which put me back to stage one...
So some land came into view...
And that's bout tha time that I met you...
I didn't even know what to do...
Till you proved you to be true...
I thank my God for your love...
Cause all the hatred I received...
Had me stuck in stage one...
And I almost didn't believe...
That I would break all the shackles...
All the chains around my neck...
Till God made me black Samson...
Then hatred gave me respect...
Now I look for the sun/son...
Cause I know tomorrow it'll gone come
I won't even try to run...
Thank God for the special one...

The Mastel
Copyright Mastel 2003

Through The Storm

Through the storm there are many things that can be learned to realize about self
One can realize to be thankful for surviving it as well as being thankful for good health
When I 1st started weathering storms it was kinda hard for me to take it
Cause the storm I was and been going through was a hurricane full of hatred
Lightening bolts of ignorance began to strike severely on my brain
While the roll of thunder was the beat of my heart thumping from the pain
The rain was the tears that fell from my eyes, soul, and lovemynd
But I still kept on praying, hoping, and waiting for love's (God) sun/son to shyne
When I thought that the storm couldn't get any worse a wave of hate toppled my building of roses and love
Blynded me from seeing the light and death was all I could think of
"Am I dying is this the end when will this agony and pain just stop and go away"
Or is this feeling of not being wanted or needed is this feeling really here to stay
Not today my soul cries and from afar someone heard my soul cry so very aloud
Someone who I consider my hero and became that rainbow ribbon to smile my cloud proud
Now after the storm I looked hopelessly for real roses (love) beneath every step of my toes
And I almost tripped up and passed it by but fell cause here a rose grows
The rose it represents you cause you're the most beautifulest jewel in this poem
I thank God extremely cause I never knew that a rose could grow through the storm

The Mastel
Copyright Mastel 2003

I met Hatred Riding a Horse but Love picked me up in a Cadillac

I was walking down the street of natural life one-day
And saw a steed of horses traveling straight ward my way
The 1st one was blue hatred, which had 2 horns as like a bull
And behind him were ignorance, lust, and jealousy that he'd always pull
I began to run because of what I thought that they could do to me
But that was yellow ignorance the 2nd horse still not being true to me

I Met Hatred Riding a Horse but Love picked me up in a Cadillac

The 3rd and most beautiful horse was the horse called green lust
This horse was so beautiful that I stopped running to ride giving it my full trust
I was on it for a short while until jealousy, which was white and had a white night
Then 3 more horses appeared with wings seeming as if to strike and take flight
The leader was Rose love a red horse with the mane of a lion
And the pink horse Power Princess answered we've arrived with perfect timing

I Met Hatred Riding a Horse but Love picked me up in a Cadillac

Now the 3rd horse with wings was brown with a crown surrounding a unicorn horn
This horse was called Wisdom knowledge and told me that there was a king that was born
A king that drove a Cadillac it was a Coupe de ville called Heaven
And that he was following them and would be there shortly to pick me up around about 7
7 colors on 7 horses and a king in a Cadillac coming at 7 o'clock
But Wisdom knowledge told me that I would need a key to unlock the lock

I Met Hatred Riding a Horse but Love picked me up in a Cadillac

Now love was the king and the king was love that had a Cadillac full of people
And everyone in the Cadillac was very beautiful and knew love all as an equal
The chrome of the Cadillac was made out of diamonds and shined whenever it would pass you bye
But young mynded me didn't know that I had had the key and the key to ride was to die
Now this story is whole because the story is told for myndz that wanna relax and slack
Just a few wordz of how I met hatred riding a horse but love picked me up in a Cadillac

The Mastel
Copyright Mastel 2003

Once Upon a Time...

Once upon a time there was a strong black man
He met this woman and tried to love her as fast as he can
She didn't know love so she didn't know how to receive
Love from the good man nor did in God she believe
She had a rocky childhood, which made her too rocky to understand
That in order to receive love and respect you must first love a good man
Not to mention the kids the strong man had before they made love so wild
But I gotta say that this particular woman didn't know love so she hated his childs
She was jealous because of the love that was born in him and them continued to fuse
And since she didn't know love again she tried to make the strong man choose
Choose her and he would win but choose his kids and then he would lose
She couldn't understand that that was abuse and that abuse left the man confused
He tried to look pass the eve (il) desire that burned hellishly in the woman's heart
But the woman did not want togetherness she only wanted things to grow apart
She had a third child for the man and tried to divide him even more
At this point he didn't know if he had found an angel or was he loving a whore
So as time passed the strong man grew weak and began to become Adam
Every woman that had straps nice shape forbidden fruits he had had em
The 1st 2 children were ousted out so he begin to separate his household time
Tryin to spend tyme with her and his kids away grew stress around his mynd
He almost died several tymes going back and forth between her and his eyes
And those several tymes he was near death her heart would say why won't his life just dies
Her mynd was treacherous as she wished him death for them to be extremely apart
It was almost like pharaoh when Moses said love and pharaoh just hardened his heart
The lord was with him as tyme passed and made him strong in the likening of Samson
And since her wish of his death did not come she tried to hold his child for a ransom
She also made several attempts to have him in chains since death wouldn't fulfill her hatred
Even though sometimes wrong he wrote poems sang songs and was blessed like his grandfather David
Tyme flew more he still had battle cause her hatred was like cancer diseases
He told her in the past to look with his eyes so that she could learn more about Jesus

You see Jesus was the good man spoken of earlier on if you could understand this true-life testimony
If it's all about you you need to learn to be true because hatred will make you a phony

The Mastel
Copyright Mastel 2003

Our Father (For kids & others)

Our Father who art in heaven God is your only name
We thank you dear God for this here life and that your son came
The kingdom is yours on heaven and on earth forever and a day
Our prayers against snares and Satan who tears our myndz and spirits away
We thank you for love and your example of how we should learn, live, and listen
Forgive us dear God cause tryin is hard and thank you for making us Christians

The Mastel
Copyright Mastel 2003

Pains of Rain (School kids Prayers)

I wake up every morning praying to God for hugs
Because as a child at school I see young people with drugs

I wish things could change cause I know it ain't right
Why is so many young people not listening and want to fight

Maybe one day our parents and family will stop and teach us
To follow better examples and not learn ignorant features

We ask of prayers from you the church to see the truth of God's light
To help us shyne in the darkness regardless of godless insight

Its up to us together to make a difference in this life change
So thank you dear God for taking all our sins and painz of rain

Amen

The Mastel
Copyright Mastel 2003

The Cause of my Effect part 1

From the beginning of tyme to the thoughts that come through my neck
It's been understood even in the bible that you are the cause of my effect
Eve (whisper il) was Adam's cause to the effect of him making a certain decision
Jezebel was the cause to effect an entire nation's God vision
Delilah was the cause to expose the effect of her husband Samson losing his strength
And everyone know that without Sarah it was impossible for Abraham to go the whole length
That's why it's a must that I write to us what is embedded inside of me
To encourage the real meaning of love for all families to see
My mother and father were the initial cause to the effect of a continued spiritual mynd
And a blessed black woman caused the effect of love to a physical kynd
You see you might not know what it is you do that causes the effect of my hearts direction
But we humans are influential people that causes effect on each other's perception
Husbands, wives, mothers, fathers, cousins, sisters, grannies, and brothers
We were put here for a reason to cause the effect of one another
A good woman and I mean a good woman has the power to cause her family to have an extreme positive effect
While the only effect that a negative woman has is mainly to cause division, chaos, and a household to shipwreck
A godly focused man with a good godly woman they could die right now and heaven is on their side
While a broken man supported by an evil woman they only make hell their place to hide
You see black women you are the cause of my effect rather you like it or not
You are the one that's able to cause a cool over me whenever my soul grows hellish and hot
You're able to keep me strong unlike Delilah did for the champion Samson
And whenever I'm wrong and ugly its you that dresses me better to make my heart right and handsome
You can control the universe black queen if you could only see these words as proverbs of light to your mynd
Oh yeah you are the cause to my effect for all of our suns/sons to live love and to shyne

Black man I ain't forgot about you you have some effects that you have caused yourself that has affected our people
I blame you and me for not showing our women how to love us them and all of us equal
You are the blame cause you just want to whore get unsober and consider it all just part of a <u>game</u>
Well black male race your eyes are crooked and you are wrong and I want you to let these words teach and tame
Your mynd and your zipper not to forgot about you strippers
But we need to stop playing so much and become household leader whippers
Lead these women the right way that's if you have one that wants to be lead
Cause some of them don't want to grow up they want to be spoon-fed
Like a child cause they are childish and yes you all are like that as products of a cycle
Tell me what will it hurt to try some church have your families reading the bible
Cause if you know God you know peace and you can alleviate conflict problems and stress
You can begin to understand him or her and begin to see that you both are truly blessed
Blessed to have each other so please cherish this time with all godly wisdom and respect
I told yall in this part 1 that you were the cause to my effect

The Mastel
Copyright Mastel 2003

Lyrical Insight (the 7th chamber)

May I be as bold as well as polite
To speak to your night some lyrical insight
In the first chamber of my mynd
There appears an eternal myndshyne
In the second chamber of my heart
I see fake love meant to fall apart
In my third chamber soulfully speaking
I see promises of Moses and them peaking
My fourth chamber is simple and plain
Like drops of rain I try to run in between my pain
Oh yes… the Fifth chamber is next
My favorite activity that ends with a X
Then its six written on my over all agenda
I think about love's warmth and also love's very cold winter
My 7th chamber is wide a number I can never divide
The angels are coming the angels are coming
Can you tell me where we can hide…

The Mastel
Copyright Mastel 2003

Please Strengthen my Try

My life is torn...
Sometimes it seems fake...
Am I really existing like the matrix...
Or am I living a mistake...
Time seems shorter...
Maybe it's the end of my living...
Will death be abrupted...
Will my soul be forgiven...
I think about all that have left before me...
Years ago and recently...
How long do I have left...
Will I leave here descent or indecently...
My household is destroyed...
More battles than it is necessary...
I'm perplex by hatred...
So much that I envision early the cemetery...
A while I've not seen my creations...
Then again I'm in no shape to train them...
I think if I was around them all...
The way I've been living would just shame them...
The one that I am around now...
Man I'm a parental vandal...
Doing the things that I am doing constantly...
Is the perfect bad example...
I can't tell girls no...
And just keep a discipline focus in my brain...
Looking at the family God gave me...
This ain't what they showed me...
This ain't how I was trained...
Pop's a preacher mom tried to keep me right...
And I still ended up in jail...
If not listening to some of their advice got me then...
Continuing to be stubborn will have me locked up in hell...
Where the devil dwells and no love is shown at all for people to see...
Where's my life going ...
This recent turmoil has me seeing my own life a mystery
An unsolved mystery of life...
I guess I've been living a hustle...
Shaming my mom dem household...

Cause for right now I living in they house with a weakened muscle...
Guide me now dear Lord...
Cause just like in that car I'm spinning out of control about to die...
I don't even know where to start at dear Lord...
Please guide me and strengthen me and my try...
The Mastel
Copyright Mastel 2003

If You Rush Your Mynd...

If you rush your mynd you won't be able to see the blue skyline
This is just a sweet lil message remindin you in life to take your time
Cause true love if rushed will be extremely hard to find
And if you rush my emotions all infatuation will do is blynd
Block out true feelings and give false feelings of us together
You see the same similitude with the changing of the weather
The sun is out but its still gonna be a rainy day today
That's what happens when you rush thoughts too in the same exact way
It's almost like rushing a wish to happen or rushing God with a prayer
Think about heaven God's kingdom do you really have authority up there
I mean can you really make God do something when you say do it
Then stop and think about human life when you try to rush me to it
Rushing on the highway can and will possibly lead to a death of human life
And if you rush like Samson, Ahab, and the rest (myself) you could choose the wrong wife
Rush rush rush why are you so much in a hurry for
Don't you know rushing sex will chance you to catch HIV much more
Something else about rushing and this is going to get ready to close this story
If you are made to judge rushing your mynd could wrong me before you even know me
All in all rushing is no good cause what you're rushing to will probably be there till the ending of your time
And you won't be able to make any and I mean any sound judgments if you rush your mynd

Mastel
Copyright Mastel 2003

Hatred Romantic #7

Romance me with hatred seems like the fate of my mynd, spirit, and heart
I didn't wanna dance with you oh beautiful hatred why couldn't we just meet and then us depart
Cause the love we made produced 7 deaths for 7 eyes beyond 7 starz in grayish blue skies
And out those skies came down painz of rain which made 7 sun's/son's eyes cries
The 1st cry was for your enemy love at least 75% to the positive in planet earth
And the 2nd cry came from no compassion cause compassion had met the death of its birth
The 3rd cry from the 4th sun/son roared against anger and mankind'z love for your child ignorance
The 4th cry from the 1st sun/son was because no one would have faith or believe in the prince
The 5th and 6th cry kinda go hands in hand cause lust, jealousy, and envy really does kill a man
If you lust after a romance with hatred your jealousy will make you envy chaotic evil then death is in your hand
Kill me #7 cause this is what our romance was about me wanting to cheat with love's heaven
The 7th sun/son had that 7th cry against a Hatred Romantic #7

The Mastel
Copyright Mastel 2003

The Reason that I am...

Who would have ever known that you would be the one to become my mother
The one who would love me through all troubles and pains like no other
The one who sacrificed to be with me when dad was not always there to hear me whine
You comforted my soul whenever my heart felt like or feels like crying
God gave me to you and you gave me God and all your heart
Taking time up to raise me wasn't an easy job but you did more than your part
Even though I gave you a hard time sometimes you were determined to stay
The mother of a child who made you a mother on your very first mother's day
I guess I'm the 1st reason that you are a mother and you are the real reason that I exist
And I'll never really be able to thank you for even considering doing this
Cause it took a lifetime to raise me but you stuck it out through the thick, the thin, and then some
Can you remember like my Mary the time when I was just one
2,3,4,5,6, and all the ages past 7 and 8
Do you remember all those times when you were tired but you still fixed me a hot plate
Even when I was close to death, sick, or hurting in pain
Thank you woman...because you were there when no one else came
Making sure that I had everything I needed from daycare to entering into high school
And oh yeah thanks for taking that belt to whip me whenever I acted like a big fool
I guess I have to say that you are truly the reason that I exist...you never thought abortion
You are the reason that I know life, you were in mines a great portion
All the way to the end and there is no one else that ever could, would, or can
Be all the things that you are to me especially the reason that I am...

Thanks Mom for having me

Happy Mother's Day 2002
By Druce Rouzan

Copyright Druce 2002

Blanket of love...

Thank you God for saving me from my being lonely
When there was no one else who would you atoned me
You gave supported and have always known me
And if it wasn't for you I could not have grown me
This extra strong tree of my life that is on me
In and out and ain't no choice you gotta be the only
That stayed for real when everyone else acted phony
I extremely want to thank you for your love you have always shown me
Thank you again for the blanket of love that you keep on putting on me...

Blanket of love...

The Mastel
Copyright Mastel 2006

Consideration 101

A teenage girl has sexual relations with a married man
She has no stability don't know where her baby will live and land
Her parents try to reach out with love to give her a helping hand
She's trying to grow up herself so she's not strong enough to take a stand
Man, and...her brothers and sisters they have some issues and eyes too
The little sisters are looking like monkey see you monkey wanna go and do
The boys are like my click wants me to be hard and real but true
And dad is like please everybody believe that God loves me and you
And wife too...speaking of wife she's stuck in a neutral but steady zone
Most of her social tyme is spent talking to family and friends on the phone
When the children need her affection she be "please just leave me alone"
Dad be like why you want us to be at home if we ain't about to get it on...
Aw man its on...here comes the fussing, cussing, fightin, and arguments
Its chaos in the residence hatred generated can't make sense
It's like the dirty spirits in this building need a spirit rinse
But the host can't get close they all became very dense every since no repentance
Tense is the new lifestyle child that they adopted there
Now everybody walkin around like they just don't give a care
You get and I don't get hatred growed it some brand new hair
From the momma to daddy to the sons and daughters don't you think consideration is fair
Oh well moving forward on to fix these simple made situations
The God said "it takes me to cure all of these complications"
The biggest word that was missing and still has been given misplacing
That we all have failed to use, what's the word CONSIDERATION...

Consideration 101
The Mastel
Copyright Mastel 2006

To My Own...

Dwindling down the tunnel of hate to meet my fate
Beggin for love and compassion to procreate
A new life become a husband to its wife
And never divide erase the existence of the knife
Kill strife with a pen like Christ's blood killz sin
Forgive me Lord, for the crowd that I chose to live in
Cause soon I'll be gone all alone with no phone
Thank God for his home where I can be to my own...

Mastel
Copyright Mastel 2004

Blue Moon, Red Sky, Purple Sun/Son

It's only once in a Blue Moon that you see a Red Sky and Purple Sun/Son
On this particular day I saw all 3 and not just 1
The sky was Red because of all the blood boil of hatred
And the Purple Sun/Son shyned royalty from the remnants of King David
The grass was still green from the green storm that had just passed
And the ocean had become a swamp from all the death that had amassed
The ocean's discolor waz from the mostly dead having black skin
And the moon waz cold and Blue because of seeing all of the white sin
The night was considered white and the day was known as black
And Love was finally on the way in the coupe de ville Cadillac
On this day all mankind and myself were afraid of leaning of all of our fates
For we were unsure if we would learn hell or belong in the Pearly Gates
Yellow lightening struck killing those who loved and enjoyed ignorance
And the Red Sky devoured them and the swamp like some smoke from some incense
Demons began to erupt standing twice the sizes of man
Then Angels of Thugz came and I knew that war waz in the land
The Earth had stopped spinning because it had rolled its way to the Sun/Son
The sky turned into fire and the mortals began to run
Humans were crying aloud but there was no noise that could be heard
And everything evil had lost its fight cause the Sun/Son was the final Word
Death had been put on its final mission God's Word waz in position
And everything from a flea to a he and she were killed if not a Christian
Discipline and Order was now and judgment had already begun
This waz the only day in my life I saw a Blue Moon, Red Sky Purple Son/Sun

The Mastel
Copyright Mastel 2003

How Could I Forget about God?

What has happened to me and my life…?
Why has things gotten so hard…
How did I become addicted to weed…?
How could I forget about GOD…?
I watch myself now as I…
Spiral downward to complications…
And sometimes it becomes a thought…
I could probably fix these situations…
Maybe I could change my life…
I could divide the evil from my soul…
I guess I live for my friendz approval…
That's why I ain't got no self-control…
I don't have any control over my life…
I mean no me control at all…
I think because I might get laughed at…
I'm afraid if I stand I might just fall
I don't know why I'm scared of falling…
Cause I've fell/failed sometimes before…
Had a chance to walk with GOD…
And all these extremities I did ignore…
I need to remind myself it's not cool…
To be even with them but odd…
So much running through my mynd…
But how did I forget about GOD…

To be continued…

The Mastel
Copyright Mastel 2004

I Broke My Own Heart

I broke my own heart by not listening to God
It ripped me apart how I filled us with darts
Know he told me to build the ark to guide us from the dark
I didn't play my part living this wasn't smart
He told me how to live my life with positive
We need remember this cause you get what you give
And if you give God your hate no love you create
And on the judgment date hell will be your fate
Cause fakin it with God will make your life hard
Its good to be odd forgive me God cause I broke my own heart

The Mastel
Copyright Mastel 2004

Chapter 4...

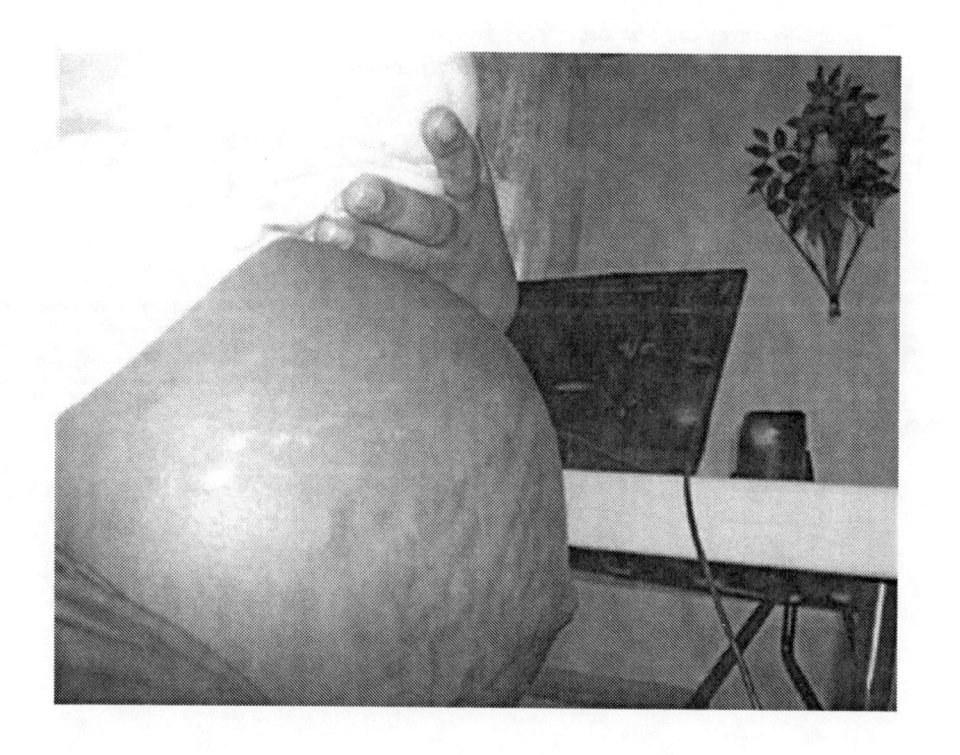

There's always a beginning to every end

Spiritual Felonies

From iniquities to my antiquities my God has been forgiving me's
Some victories wasn't meant 2 be which brought on me some miseries
For my friendz and my enemies to the unknowns that envies me's
Here's a quick story clearing all my spiritual felonies
With felonies they be tellin me's stained forever in the counturies
Those lies with more evil seeds lets me know its only God we needs
From this country to them other seas 1 God has no memories
Once the I have apologized for my spiritual felonies

Mastel
Copyright Mastel 2004

Living and Dying @ The Same Time

While I'm here living I'm dying this comes without @ all trying
Its like freezing while frying pressure is released while it's applying
I was born to die tell me how ironic is that
I work hard for a short while and then my life turns black
30 to a hundred years only minutes in his eye
sometimes we stand just to sit and watch life pass us by
I'm living to die sometimes I say why do I even try
I mean I'm thankful for the opportunity but sometimes I live a lie
The lie that I live runs my mynd through the negative
And the proof living truth is I let be dead energy that's positive
Now if that energy was kinetic then my mynd would over shine
But since its still potential energy my life is wasting its time
I got years left then I don't have much time left @ all
Cause eventually through life that I stand death will make me fall
Time iz increasing and decreasing @ the immediate speed of my mynd
We all begin to end and we're living and dying @ the same time

The Mastel
Copyright Mastel 2004

The Faith and Confidence Killer

I am the one when you are pain stricken that lusts to pain U more
The one that fathers fear and envy the one that hatred loves to adore
I am the one that sees clearly when you are weary with your faith in God
The one that knows that you hurt already but I still make your hurt hurt hard
The one that when you are ill I destined to prove to make you iller
I am your worster than worst nightmare I am your faith and confidence killer

The Mastel
Copyright Mastel 2003

How Did I become Jesus?

How did I become Jesus man, somebody was already chose to do that. I guess people need somebody else to accuse or blame for their faults with their visions...

All these accusations, false judgments, miss-guidance that come from bad features
Makes a person like me wonder and plunder, how did I become Jesus?
There was only one Jesus that was said to have already came
He came to heal your lames with his name but folks still used him for blame
He has been the center focal point for all things considered boastful bad or greatly good
In his time he was known by his close friends and family as the one who did and always could
Save them from tragedy, bring joy to their hearts, souls, and myndz
But they had hatred worst than against David because his spirit waz like one of those of no kindz
He was considered for blame cause when he spoke truth it failed the self-righteous men'z lies
He was also blamed wrong for his right when he gave people Love from God's Eyes
He was constantly accused over and over by men who believed only in their lies and own self-opinions
When they not knowing that the future held death for all by an opinion that over alls other's dominions
Never the less he met death by the hands of his own family and supposed friendz
That's why I ask now to you that have odd starz in your family what do you really intends
To kill their spirit with your ill spirit or with judgmental diseases
I see now that probably through my actions and how you with your actions how we can all have chance to become Jesus

Mastel
Copyright Mastel 2004

Adversity

Adversity is challenge a hurdle or interruption
It could be temptation on the whole an annoying life disruption
Adversity is opposition against any mynd'z position
It can also be looked upon as a form of mental nutrition
My adversity has a team with 7 different players
They tried to stop parts of my life but I always had me a savior
A savior who was a king that strengthened these wordz in me against enemy
Thank God for this building block that they call adversity

The Mastel
Copyright Mastel 2003

What!!!! are you lookin for

What!!!! are you lookin for
Are you lookin to see if I am a whore
Are you lookin to see if God gave you more
Are you lookin to see if you can make me poor
Or are you lookin to see how God makes me soar
Makes me roar his love I do adore
What is it really in me that you are lookin for
Are you lookin to see if I can go back to the me before
Are you lookin to see if it is true about all the hatred that came I bore
Are you lookin to see if through the pressure my spirit became tore
Or are you lookin to see if your ignorance my soul will ignore
Are you lookin to see if you can reign/rain on over me galore
Are you lookin to see if God stayed the land to my shore
Are you lookin to continue on with your self-righteousness against my forever more
Tell me in all seriousness… what in God's name are you lookin for

Mastel
Copyright Mastel 2005

Why do Daddies Die?

Why do daddies die?
So you can get a chance to let your emotions cry
See how pretty their wings grow when they die and fly
You're gonna get your chance soon believe me and that's no lie
To spread your wings too and soar through the God's heavenly sky
That's the reason why daddies die
So they can make heaven's rooms multiply
So that when you get there love and your space will be in place in full supply
Here's some tissue for your emotions your tears need to be dry
Are you sad that I'm gone mad and alone can't figure out the reason why
There's no answer for you cause that chase you could never satisfy
That's why I told you so long until later instead of farewell or goodbye
Why do you even try cause this is life and then death, I had to comply
We can still see each other when we both look with a closed unopened eye
I mean I'm in your mynd you're in my mynd God is all we need to apply
To dissipate your sometime questions of why do daddies die

The Mastel
Copyright Mastel 2004

To my good friends in which both lost their fathers, yall know who you are and to anybody else that lost a father or a loved one use this to help understand the reason why we die. Thank you.

Wait on God's will...

I'm on the verge to submerge my pistols got the urge
To shoot no refute cause my rent needs loot
Got no job so I rob stick and move on a bob
Take the cash runnin fast hope I don't have to blast
1st I flip a new script cause the God is equipped
With a shyne greatest mynd came in right on time
Don't have to steal wait on his will God gave me his shield
Against the devil became that rebel to those thoughts unreal

God's will...God's will...God's will (2Xs)
Wait on God's will...
To be revisited and extended

The Mastel
Copyright Mastel 2005

The Christian Relationship Story (example)

There was this one woman...
Who could have very possibly had some chance
To embrace a player's heart fully...
Make him dance to her romance
She wasn't the most beautifulest thing to kiss
But she had some few mental attractions
She always kept the relationship pissed...
With her stupid mynd'z distractions
She always questioned love without really letting it be
It was like she wanted a real relationship but
Wouldn't let control of it be free
She'd constantly challenge the man with questions
And her ignorance from within
Then she'd judge him to be the enemy when he
Wanted to be her friend
She tried to teach their kids too,
That that was the way to live
Not teaching kids constructively was why
They judged a good man negative
Advice was given to the young woman but she
Let the devil miss-guide her mynd
She said she wanted a Christian man I guess
Because she wanted to crucify him all the time
Maybe not knowing, naw that's a lie, she knew
Cause she was always assuring she was grown
And she always thought she could demand love
And respect through speaking a loud tone
Proverbs 15:1 says to us folks clearly how to
Get respect from any situation
That in order to get good respect we must
<u>Tone</u> down our presentation
We must know humility whenever we go
On our relationship missions
But 1st and foremost it takes a Christian
Woman to get love/respect from a man that's a Christian

The Mastel
Copyright Mastel 2005

Thank Q. keep it comin

Search Your Soul...

Search your soul...
2 gain control...
2 fix yourself 2 make U whole...
If not you belong inside a commode...
With human feces U R a load...
Won't change your rush...
The ignorant touch...
Its hurting other humans 2 much 2 much...
You'll stop not roll...
If you don't console...
Do it 4 your sake and search your soul...

Mastel
Copyright The Mastel 2005

The Pleasure in my Pain

I pleasure in my pain because all my pain is here to train
My mynd, spirit, and soul to realize from pain growz gain
Cause if I did not have pain there would be no sun/son after the rain
And if there was no ignorance then how could hatred be entertained
If there was no murder, how could Christ have ever been slained
And if I wasn't Lil Black Horner the white governments couldn't give me strain
If there were no problems then how or what could humans complain
Without my pain I'd be praisin some glory to a God in vain
Without pain I think that too perfect people would probably go insane
Cause they couldn't judge other people to make them become a stain
All of this is said cause there is a God whose love it will remain
Beyond this world's immaturity I enjoy the pleasure in my pain

The Pleasure in my Pain
The Mastel
Copyright Mastel 2003

Thank God for this Dream...
(this is one of my visions)

All of a sudden it came...rain pouring down the veins of my heart
Speaking of heart, my heart's thumping thunder on its way of falling apart
What does this pain mean...is death becoming my new state of existence
And when death is me, does my life have a continued lifetime persistence
Is death really the opposite of life or is it a somewhat extension
Here's the touch chapter, the ghost chapter of an ideal vision...
I waz driving down the street one day watching an extreme and perfect sky
When 2 pearly gates amazingly appeared and opened up before my Eye
I didn't know what waz happening...waz this a scene from a future dream
Then appeared a mansion and a bunch of beings smiling bright with wingz
The appearance of earth changed when the sky waz rearranged
And the street in which I waz traveling became golden and kinda strange
The street waz so beautiful that I wanted to stop to travel on feet
Because for as long as I had lived I had never seen such a street
The street waz a maze with signs stating to give God praise
I still waz wondering if I waz daydreaming and stuck in a daze
Then I saw a light in the sky I thought that maybe the light waz God
But it waz a star, the ultimate star, that waz born considered odd
I looked back behind me to see what the earth had become
And the earth waz redder than mars with much fire and then sum
As a matter of fact it waz boiling as if to cook a soul till it waz done
And the street became stairs while I began to run toward the son/sun

The Mastel
Copyright The Mastel 2006

Take Heed to God'z Advice...

Was it because my mynd was too deep
Or was it because my jolly personality would not sleep
It had to be something either questionable or marvelous indeed
Because their, why, questions interviewed me so constantly and urgent for need
If there were answers or not their hearts were quite needy for sure
When I only had one why question really... why can't you jus love me humbly more
More love through the humility that they would present with certain selected persons
The more God and myself pleaded for tenderness the more their contentious ways worsen
It's almost like the pharaoh and Moses when the God said let my people go
But pharaoh hardened his heart even more when he would viciously say no
Or like myself I should say when I was pleaded to stop my evil ways against God and myself
Drinking, smoking, fornication I thought it was good but it was bad for my health
God had asked me to release those things so that me as his people could myself be free
But all I did was run even harder to those death traps full of iniquity
But back to these persons because this story has a spiritual moral goal
When you present a one sided of unpleasantness to certain people you heap more punishments upon your soul
Your soul becomes human scorn/scumb living in hell beggin for God'z heavenly ice
Cause you wouldn't be nice humble like Christ and you wouldn't take heed to God'z advice

Mastel
Copyright Mastel 2005

It's Been a While...

Its like my mynd had just woke up...
Then again maybe it was that my God got mad and spoke up
He said Mastel where is your mynd...
My mynd spoke back on its own
My faithful and always honest lord
I'm right here spending tyme in the between lost and confused zone
In an involuntary way I asked will you please rescue me from my ignorance...
He answered back...I have...
But in dealings with the devil is where you have your persistence
Then he left me with the answer of salvation that had already been given
Then I began my soul search to see if I could honestly recall how I was living
What I reviewed in my memories immediately made me ashamed
Cause seemibly almost every evil that was generated my soul had listed and named
I asked myself... why did you do all of this very un-godly unrighteousness
Instead of thanking the most high for sending his most valuable preciousness and priceless ness
My soul had no answer but looked at my mynd and my spirit with huge clouds of sorrow
Wishing that there was some kinda happiness that I could borrow until it was tomorrow
(Chuckle) borrowing some happiness till I could see some happiness later
What kinda mentality was given to me from my spiritual and human creator
Nevertheless I began to realize that the more I freed the hatred that I had captured
The more that the spirit of God in me his love began to spread and manufacture
A brightness which was the son/sun making the clouds of living the world dissipate
So then the more I freed love from its prison the more I freed all of the incarcerated hate
Freeing both at the same tyme increased a somewhat elementary knowledge that I should've already knew
And the closer I got to God (the reading of his word) the more my soul grew to become true...
True to myself first then to him and others, which made my insides, and out shyne a beautiful smile
I see now that I should have been been talking to my God...and that it was true...its been a little while...

The Mastel
Copyright The Mastel 2006

Look Behind you 2 find you...

Look behind you 2 find you...
Your past is 2 remind you...
If you re-live you, you rewind you...
Satan's curse has unshyned you...
You change, friends they never do mind you...
And if they do, they do it 2 trap you and to tyme you...
Be strong and overlook them so you can design you...
And don't let their hatred enter you to unclimb you...
Instead let Jesus' perfect love heart valentine you...
With the love that God wants to intertwined you...
Cause these fake friendz pretend you just 2 blind you...
God's thoughts look behind you 2 find you...

The Mastel
Copyright The Mastel 2005

Building a House to tear it down

Build a house 2 tear it down
Is like making a sentence that has no nouns
It's like making a smile turn into a frown
Its like jumping into water to swim wishing 2 drown
Or like buying some speakers hating the sound of sound
Or like loving the circus hating everything down 2 the clown
Or like winning a King/Queen ship hating 2 wear the crown
Or like working hard 2 build a family with loving ignorance 2 B around…

I saw an example of which so I must speak a short story
About how this 1 magnificent person spoke God but down played his glory
This person spoke good things 2 encourage but rattled satan-like right after
Which made me wonder which persona was this person considering their master
Was it God or the devil because they had jus gave some beautiful advice
But turned around and put me down faster than falling on a sheet of grease and ice
They had made someone a breakfast way better than some good restaurant food
But made the person not want it at all because of their afterwards attitude
Good intentions gone bad makes you happy then you're sad
Why why why if you're a friend why do you talk so mad
You've built a heart up with an image 2 B loved and sought after
Then U tear things apart with your mynd'z flipped out disaster
I saw a strong supportive woman 1 time design the perfect home for bragging
She had attracted a good man but pushed him away with all of her nagging
She'd always complain questioning every blessing that God gave her
And even though there was a Jesus she wanted strife to save her
All in all to end this story her hearts happiness could never B found
Cause she used the goodness God gave her 2 build a house that she beg satan 2 tear down.

The Mastel
Copyright Mastel 2005

(Needs to be rewritten putting thoughts in proper places along with patterns. Incomplete)

Y Iz Your Hat Red?

Why is your hat red... some wonder why this statement was said
Probably because the wearing of this could leave human bodies dead
Nevertheless I try my best to fight hard against stress
Because swallowing a red hat would be extremely hard to digest
Hard in deed because who knows what is to come later on after
When the conclusion of reading love's book and hate is the final chapter
Do you really know what hate extends later on to become or be
It becomes the very growth to stop your mynd from being happy and free
Free from the sin, lies, and everything that is hateful against God
Jesus I tried... Lord you know I've been tryin real real hard
Hard to guide the souls and mynds of us a misdirected people
But I feel so tired now my Lord ... of cleaning up all our fecal
To all that say they love God and wear 2 hats on top of their head
Take the pretend one off and tell me... Y Iz Your Hat Red?

The Mastel
Copyright Mastel 2005

What Are You Doing with What God Gave You

The question that iz asked today could possibly encourage you, touch you, or even could save you
The question asked iz... "What are you doing with what God gave you"
God gave you a family... are you encouraging humility or hostility
God gave you opportunity do you kill your chances or push possibility
He (God) gave you Christ to give you directions for life and God'z advice
What are you doing with his gentleness do you present a meanness or iz your persona nice
Your presence to a certain few how do they like you around
Are you building God'z house or are you trying to tear it down
Don't answer these questions to me but to God cause there's many more blessings that you do receive
God gave you a faith in him... are you doubtful or do you believe
God gave you everyday of love are you interrupting them with conflict and contention
Are you balancing patience, compassion, and frustration your only dimension
He gave you a mouth and the power of speech how are you using your tone
Are you speaking softly like the proverbs or yelling cause you don't have a microphone
All these thoughts present some self-soul searching that could really help you to behave you
So now think about your other blessings and what you are doing with what God gave you

The Mastel
Copyright Mastel 2005

Who will be the Hate-est

When things get complicated
I feel like the king known as David
Because of what others generated
The little bad word called hatred
Sometimes it's hard for me to take it
So I won't lie and try to fake it
My brain, folks try to bake it
But my God didn't leave me naked
He sent me his best the greatest
To clothe me with the latest
But hatred begins to multiply
Now who will be the hatest?

The Mastel
Copyright Mastel 2005

A Higher Love

I gotta question I gotta ask… when you look at me…
My outsides, my insides… what do you think of
Do you think of me as a lesser me or of me as a higher love
What part of me do you know well enough to describe
My heart's entire description
Is a one-sided you seeing a one-sided me am I 1-D
Is this your only depiction
Well guess what I am 1-D meaning only one-D
But I have a variety of characteristics involved
Meaning there iz only one me but there are different
Human instincts around my one soul that revolves
But what I am talking about I know to you it might be
Strange
Maybe after reading this peace I hope that your <u>confusions</u>
Do change
I was born an innocent soul not knowing to judge or to be
Judged by other people
From my 1stness of learning, seeing you seeing me
I considered our myndz different but us equal
Actually right now I still do believe that to be the truth
That my God has sent to me
But by other wanna be demanding perspectives I learn that
Evil ambitions of man are very rude to me
This one statement which iz God's known fact
To those of you that wear my envied black robe
Judgment day for me iz not yet here but real death
Belongs to that judgment road
The road of death and the road of judgment can be controlled
By one strong determining factor
Master God… while all you young and old judges are then
Turned into mere actors
Why fall faint now when you really realize your harsh
Miss judging was God's hatred
Is it hard for you to face or take it or you're not strong enough
When its your turn to luv <u>you</u> complicated
Men and women I tell you all that it is the compassion in you and
Me is what you really need to be thinking of
Because it is the compassion of God that will eventually get you to
That me… that me, the Higher Love…
A Higher Love

The Mastel
Copyright Mastel 2005

Why

Why are you so sad and blue
Why won't you look forward to the new
Why won't you truly let me really rest in peace
Why are you holding on so tight and won't release
You see I left you for a reason that is difficult to explain
And I get tired of every time I hear you…you always whining my name
Me this me that when will you let me be
And just be glad that God gave you a good memory of me
Didn't we have fun together always smiling and playing
Why can't you just let go and introduce yourself to the art of prayin
Why don't you know God is real and he has total control
Of everything that exist including your broken soul
Give it to him cause he is forever my replacement
Change your heart so it can be lifted from living the basement
Life is good thank God for that good piece of wealth
And pray that you can live long and defeat bad health
Bad health spiritually physically and even mentally
Stop looking at things so deep dark and transcendentally
Stop cryin about me if you truly want to remember the rainbow
And pour in the water of Christ to quench your volcano

The Mastel
Copyright Mastel 2001

Thank God We made It...Part Two

4 the living and belated and 4 those who didn't make it
Is the example how we should C life's death and embrace it
In our thoughts not our memories a waste of some good energies
Learn we all R 1 race and not considering enemies
What...you want me 2 think we were born all gangstaz
That ain't the way we should think but I guess I should thank ya
4 the wrong way 2 follow make us evil and inside hollow
The ignorance the devil wants us 2 lust, trust, and swallow
Allow me 2 B 2 U a reminder of these iniquities
The new real Gs believe N getting down on their knees
God please 4give all of the sex and the tension
4 me not listenin pay close attention, Christian rearrange your vision
And let your mynd travel to the real and not into the shadow
God really did win the war and he did kill the battle
Against Satan that's Y his teamin demons B hatin
Cause victorious van glorious is constantly hesitatin
2 B given 2 hatred against our war physical David
The God be with us still...thank God that we made it

Thank God We made It...Part 2

The Mastel
Copywritten Mastel 2005

Look What Your Hatred's doing...

Look what your hatred's doin to you
And doin to me
It tearing us apart
But it keeps improvinin me
Makin me become strong
Become the new black Samson
But still satan has your soul
For a unforgiving ransom
It's all on you to change your heart
And begin to think smart
Your mynd is a beautiful thing
A perfect design of God's art
Why harden your heart
Pharaoh did it and felt the wrath of God
Please don't be so odd
Especially against God's heavy handed rod
You will continue to have pain
As long as you fight love (God) and entertain
Ignorance and hatred
Your life will always be complain
So maintain...

D Mastel
Copyright Mastel 2003

You and you only choose to see what you want to see

What do you see... Yourself...or me?

The Mastel

Special Thanks to everyone who help to inspire Through the Storm especially my God and my Lord and Saviour Jesus the Christ...

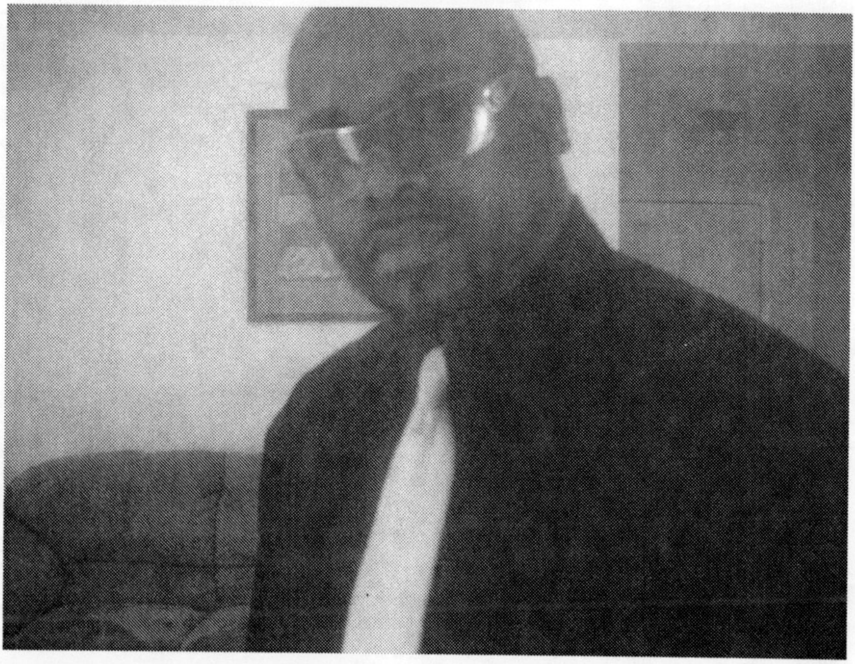

Other Books by The Mastel

1. THE MASTEL
2. A Rose for You
3. The Black Experience
4. The 7th Eye
5. The Odd Star/God Star

Printed in the United States
127676LV00004B/12/A